# Kalyakoorl, ngalak warangka

## Forever, we sing

GINA WILLIAMS & GUY GHOUSE

# Kalyakoorl, ngalak warangka

## Forever, we sing

SONGS FROM
KALYAKOORL & BINDI BINDI
ARRANGED FOR VOICE,
GUITAR AND PIANO

*Kalyakoorl, ngalak warangka, Forever, we sing,* is a celebration of Noongar language, and the things we share as community.

Over many years, Noongar language has been reduced to a whisper – today there are fewer than 400 fluent speakers. But in the same way the butterfly emerges from the cocoon, we are now witnessing a beautiful renaissance of language.

This collection of songs is from our first two albums, *Kalyakoorl, Forever* and *Bindi Bindi, The Butterfly*.

And, just like our music, this anthology is informed by the four principles of: Koort, Heart; Moort, Family and Community; Boodja, Land; and Koorlangka, Children and Legacy.

It is our hope that, through this collection of reduced scores and song sheets, our music will continue to be used in new and interesting ways, as well as shared through schools, choirs and community groups.

**Gina Williams and Guy Ghouse**

## About the authors

**Gina Williams AM** is a proud Balladong (Noongar) woman, with links through her grandmother's line to the Gija people of the East Kimberley.

She is an award-winning singer–songwriter and journalist, who has spent the past three decades committed to sharing stories and writing songs for her community. With her collaborator and best friend, Guy Ghouse, she has released three albums.

Gina was awarded the Member of the Order of Australia in 2021 for significant service to the performing arts, to Indigenous music, and to radio; she was the 2018 Inductee, West Australian Women's Hall of Fame; Winner, Aboriginal Category, 2017 West Australian of the Year; and Winner, Indigenous Act of the Year, 2013, 2014, 2015, 2016 and 2018, West Australian Music Industry Awards.

Gina is an Ambassador for the Australasian Performing Rights Association, a member of the British Council's ACCELERATE Arts and Cultural Leadership Alumni, and is a Patron of Fairbridge Folk Festival.

**Guy Ghouse** has a musical pedigree that dates back to 1920s Malaysia and there are few guitarists who connect to their music and perform without compromise like Guy.

Guy's journey has taken him all over the world, with performances at the Edinburgh Festival, Ronnie Scott's Jazz Club (UK), the BBC (UK) and the Hard Rock Cafe (UK & Indonesia), and in Los Angeles, Texas, the Netherlands and Spain.

Guy has been musical director, producer, educator, mentor for a variety of bands and solo artists, and session guitarist for many touring acts. He has written and composed for television and film.

Guy, a featured Artist with Cole Clarke Guitars, was named Winner, Best Guitarist at the 2020 West Australian Music Industry Awards.

tkoorl
a Williams and Guy Ghouse

| | |
|---|---|
| **Warangka** | **1** |
| **Kalyakoorl** | **6** |
| **Nyittiny Boodja** | **10** |
| **Nyit Yok Barnap** | **14** |
| **Balladong Worl** | **19** |
| **Maambart** | **22** |
| **Ngany Koorliny** | **25** |
| **Moordiyap** | **29** |
| **Iggy's Lullaby** | **32** |
| **Boorda** | **35** |

Wanjoo 38

Ngalak Yoowart Waahliny 44

Bindi Bindi 48

Ngany Ngaank 52

Ninnyok 59

Koorlbardi wer Wardong 62

Bilya-k 65

Benang 69

Wunding wer Wilara 74

Yeyi 78

## Warangka

Ngany koort djerap noonook kaditjiny
Noonook nganyang koordamart
Noonook nganyang koordamart
Ngany koort djerap ngalak doyntj-doyntj
Ngany koort baal warangka
Nganyang koort baal warangka

Warangka – nganyang koort
Warangka – nganyang moort
Warangka – ngalang boodja
Oooh, ngany warangka

Ngany koort djerap noonook nganyang moort
Noonook nganyang kwobidak moort
Noonook kwobidak moort
Ngalak Balladong koorlangka
Ngalang moort baalap moorditj moort
Ngalak moorditj moort

Warangka – nganyang koort
Warangka – nganyang moort
Warangka – ngalang boodja
Oooh, ngany warangka

Ngany koort djerap nidja boodja-k
Ngany moorditj boodja yoowarl-koorl
Moorditj boodja yoowarl-koorl
Ngany koorlangka bokadja koorliny
Kalyakoorl ngany Balladong
Kalyakoorl ngany Balladong

Warangka – nganyang koort
Warangka – nganyang moort
Warangka – ngalang boodja
Oooh, ngany warangka

Ngany koort djerap noonook djinanginy
Kalyakoorl ngany Balladong
Kalyakoorl ngany Balladong
(Ngany warangka, kalyakoorl warangka)
Kalyakoorl ngany Balladong
Kalyakoorl ngany Balladong

## Sing

My heart is happy at the thought of you
You are my great love
You are my great love
My heart is happy we are together
My heart, it sings
My heart, it sings

Sing – my heart
Sing – my people
Sing – our land
Oooh, I sing

My heart is happy you are my family
You are my beautiful family
You beautiful family
We are children of the Balladong
Our people are strong/solid people
We're strong/solid people

Sing – my heart
Sing – my people
Sing – our land
Oooh, I sing

My heart is happy on this land
I return to solid land
Return to solid land
My children go a long way
Forever I'm Balladong
Forever I'm Balladong

Sing – my heart
Sing – my people
Sing – our land
Oooh, I sing

My heart is happy seeing you
Forever I'm Balladong
Forever I'm Balladong
(I sing, forever sing)
Forever I'm Balladong
Forever I'm Balladong

# Warangka

## Sing

Arranged by Russell Holmes

Gina Williams and Guy Ghouse

C
G
Dm
38
ngany_wa rang - ka
Ngany koort djerap noo-nook ngan-yang moort
G
B♭maj7
43
Noo-nook ngan-yang kwo-bi-dak moort
Noo-nook kwo-bi da- k moort
B♭maj7
C
Dm
48
Nga - lak Bal-la-dong koor-lang-ka
Nga-lang
G
B♭maj7
B♭maj7
C
52
moort baa-lap moor-ditj - moort
Nga-lak moor - ditj moort
B♭maj7
C
Am7
B♭maj7
C
57
Wa-rang - ka ngan- yang - koort
Wa-rang ka ngan- yang-
G
B♭maj7
C
Am7
B♭maj7
63
moort
wa-rang- ka
nga - lang boo - dja
C
G
Dm
69
Ooh ooo
ngany Wa-rang - ka
Ngany koort djerap
G
74
ni - dja boo-dja-k
Ngany moor-ditj boo-dja yoo- warl- koorl
Moor-ditj

79
B♭maj7 B♭maj7 C Dm
bood ja yoo-warl- koorl
Ngany koor-lang-ka bok-a-dja koor-liny Kal-ya-
84
G B♭maj7 C
3
koorl ngany Ba lla dong
Kal-ya koorl ngany Ba - lla- dong
89
B♭maj7 C Am7 B♭maj7 C
Wa-rang - ka ngan- yang koort
Wa-rang ka ngan-yang -
95
G B♭maj7 C Am7 B♭maj7
moort
Wa-rang ka nga - lang boo - dja
101
C G Dm
Ooh ooo ngany wa-rang - ka
Ngany koort djerap
106
B♭maj7
3
noo-nook djin-an - giny Kal - ya - koorl nganyBal - la - dong Kal-ya
G Dm
Ngany wa-rang-ka kal - ya-koorl wa-rang-ka
koorl ngany Bal - la- dong
Ooh -

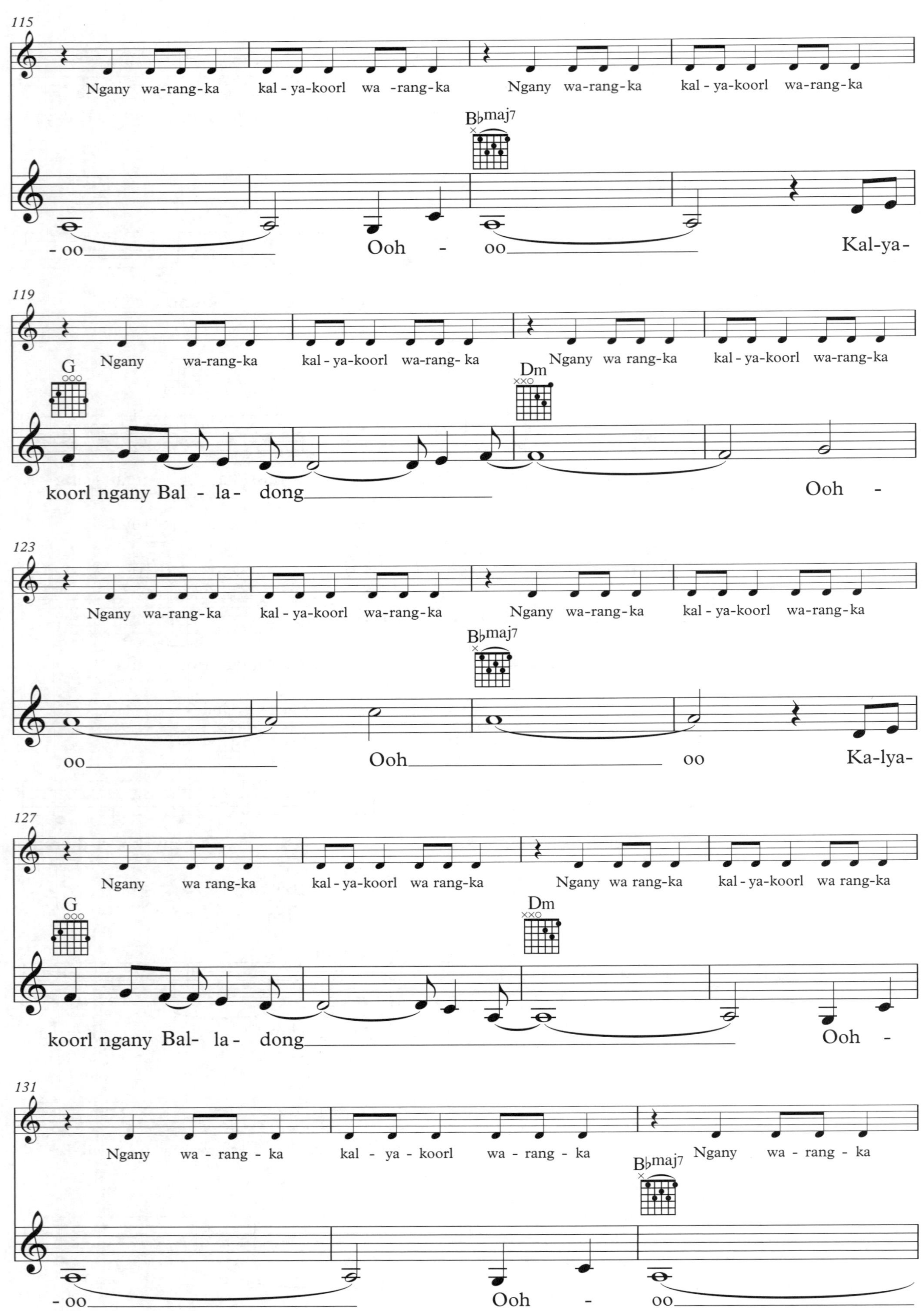
115
Ngany wa-rang-ka kal-ya-koorl wa-rang-ka Ngany wa-rang-ka kal-ya-koorl wa-rang-ka
B♭maj7
-oo Ooh - oo Kal-ya-
119
Ngany wa-rang-ka kal-ya-koorl wa-rang-ka Ngany wa rang-ka kal-ya-koorl wa-rang-ka
G
Dm
koorl ngany Bal- la- dong Ooh -
123
Ngany wa-rang-ka kal-ya-koorl wa-rang-ka Ngany wa-rang-ka kal-ya-koorl wa-rang-ka
B♭maj7
oo Ooh oo Ka-lya-
127
Ngany wa rang-ka kal-ya-koorl wa rang-ka Ngany wa rang-ka kal-ya-koorl wa rang-ka
G
Dm
koorl ngany Bal- la- dong Ooh -
131
Ngany wa-rang-ka kal-ya-koorl wa-rang-ka Ngany wa-rang-ka
B♭maj7
-oo Ooh - oo

134
kal - ya - koorl wa - rang - ka
G
kal - ya - koorl wa - rang ka
Kal - ya - koorl ngany Bal - la - dong

## Kalyakoorl

Noongar kaadak nidja boodja
Koora wer yeyi
Ngalang koorndarm baal nidja kalyakoorl
Noongar kaadak nidja boodja
Koora wer yeyi
Ngalang koorndarm baal nidja kalyakoorl

Kooba wangkiny
Ngany djaliny
Alitja noonook boola wangkiny
Bedik bedik koorliny
Boodja baal nganop
Ngany kaditjiny
Alitja baal boola djinany

Noongar kaadak nidja boodja
Koora wer yeyi
Ngalang koorndarm baal nidja kalyakoorl
Noongar kaadak nidja boodja
Koora wer yeyi
Ngalang koorndarm baal nidja kalyakoorl

Yeyi, djinany
Nidja baal
Nidja boodja baal koorang
Kedala – kedalak
Boodja-k – worl-ak
Koora koora, yeyi, benang

Noongar kaadak nidja boodja
Koora wer yeyi
Ngalang koorndarm baal nidja kalyakoorl
Noongar kaadak nidja boodja
Koora wer yeyi
Ngalang koorndarm baal nidja kalyakoorl

## Forever

Noongars have held this land
Past and present
Our dreaming is here forever
Noongars have held this land
Past and present
Our dreaming is here forever

Speak well
I am listening
There is much for you to say
Go gently
Land is still
I know
There's much to see

Noongars have held this land
Past and present
Our dreaming is here forever
Noongars have held this land
Past and present
Our dreaming is here forever

Look, now
Here it is
This earth, it turns
From day to night
Earth to the sky
Past, present, future

Noongars have held this land
Past and present
Our dreaming is here forever
Noongars have held this land
Past and present
Our dreaming is here forever

# Kalyakoorl
## Forever

Arranged by Russell Holmes

Gina Williams and Guy Ghouse

Am G Fmaj7 G Fmaj7 G
21
kaa - dak ni-dja boo - dja, Koo - ra wer yeyi Nga-lang koorn-darm baal ni - dja
A(add2) Am G Fmaj7 G
24
kal - ya- koorl Noon-gar kaa - dak ni-dja boo - dja, Koo - ra__ wer yeyi Nga-lang
Fmaj7 G A(add2) C D E Am
27
koorn-darm baal ni - dja kal-ya - koorl Yeyi dji-nany, ni - dja baal Ni-dja
C D E C D E(sus4) E Am C D
31
boo-dja ba - al__ ko- rang Ke-da - la- ke-da- lak, boodja-k wor -lak Koo-ra koo-ra, yeyi, be-
Instrumental solo
E(sus4) E Dm C B♭maj7 C B♭maj7 C D(add2) Dm C B♭maj7 C B♭maj7 C
36
na_ ng__
D(add2) F G A Dm F G A(sus4) A F G A Dm F G
44

A(add2)
Am
G
Fmaj7
G
Fmaj7
G
52
Noo - ngar kaa-dak ni-dja boo-dja, Koo-ra wer yeyi Nga-lang koorn - darm baal ni - dja
A(add2)
Am
G
56
kal - ya - koorl Noon-gar kaa - dak ni - dja boo - dja,
Fmaj7
G
Fmaj7
G
A(add2)
58
Koo - ra wer yeyi Nga-lang koorn-darm baal ni - dja kal - ya - koorl

## Nyittiny Boodja

Nyittiny boodja, baal kwobidak
Ngany koort djerabiny
Nyittiny boodja, baal kwobidak
Ngany koort djerabiny

Ngany koolark, baal kwobidak
Koolark kadjali
Ngany koolark, baal kaalang
Ngarda ngaank

Nyittiny boodja, baal kwobidak
Ngany koort djerabiny
Nyittiny boodja, baal kwobidak
Ngany koort djerabiny

Kaya! Ngany nidja
Woolah! Ngany nidja

Nyittiny boodja, baal kwobidak
Ngany koort djerabiny
Nyittiny boodja, baal kwobidak
Ngany koort djerabiny

Ngany koolark derker wardan-ak
Koorlak bokadja
Koolark boola bilya-k
Koolark bokadja

Kaya! Ngany nidja
Woolah! Ngany nidja

Nyittiny boodja, baal kwobidak
Ngany koort djerabiny
Nyittiny boodja, baal kwobidak
Ngany koort djerabiny
Nyittiny boodja, baal kwobidak
Nyittiny boodja, baal kwobidak
Nyittiny boodja, baal kwobidak
My heart is in love...

## Cold Country

Cold country, you're beautiful,
My heart is in love
Cold country, you're beautiful
My heart is in love

My home, it's beautiful
Home far away
My home, it's hot
Under the sun

Cold country, you're beautiful,
My heart is in love
Cold country, you're beautiful
My heart is in love

Yes/Hello! I'm here
Woo hoo! I'm here

Cold country, you're beautiful
My heart is in love
Cold country, you're beautiful
My heart is in love

My home is surrounded by oceans
Home way over there
Home of rivers plenty
Home way over there

Yes/Hello! I'm here
Woo hoo! I'm here

Cold country, you're beautiful
My heart is in love
Cold country, you're beautiful
My heart is in love
Cold country, you're beautiful
Cold country, you're beautiful
Cold country, you're beautiful
My heart is in love...

# Nyittiny Boodja

## Cold Country

Arranged by Russell Holmes

Gina Williams and Guy Ghouse

Am7 C D Em7 Bm7 C D
30
Ngany koort dje-ra biny Ka - ya! - Ngany nid - j-a Woo-lah!
Guitar solo
Em7 Bm7 C D Em Bm7 Am7
36
Ngany nid - ja
C D G D Bm7 C
43
2.
koolark der-ker war-dan - ak Koo-lak bok-ad - ja Koo
DSal Coda
G D Bm7 C D Em
lark boo - la bil - ya - k Koo-lark bo-ka - dja Nyit-tiny boo-dja, baal
D Am7 C Em
kwo-bi- dak, ngany koort dje - ra - biny Nyit-tiny boo-dja, baal
C D C Em
kwo - bi dak, ngany koort dje - ra - biny Nyit-tiny boo-dja, baal
D Am7 C C D D Em
kwo-bi dak, Nyit-tiny boo-dja, baal kwo-bi da - k, Nyit tiny boo-dja, baal

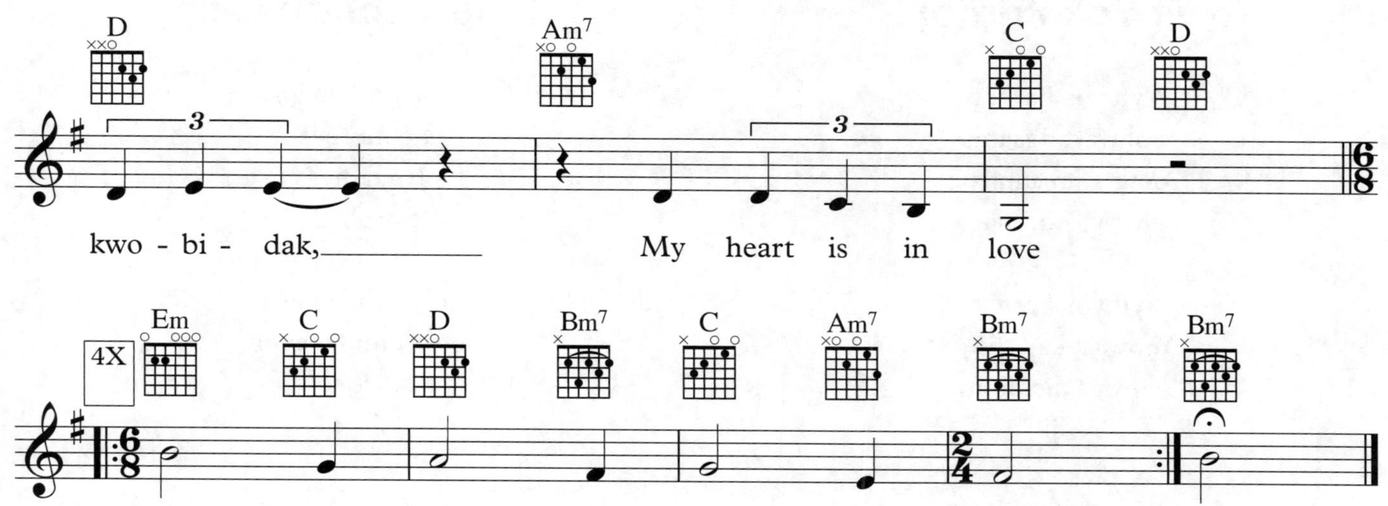
D
Am7
C
D
3
3
kwo - bi - dak,
My heart is in love
Em
C
D
Bm7
C
Am7
Bm7
Bm7
4X

## Nyit Yok Barnap

Nyit yok barnap
Yoowart ngaank
Yoowart maambart
Nyit yok barnap

Nyit yok barnap
Yoowart kaditjiny
Yoowart djerabiny
Nadjil?

Wadjella koorliny
Baal barnap yok waangkininy
Noonook yoowart ngaank
Wer maambart barang
Noonook yoowart djinany
Noonar ngaank wer maambart
Baalap kadjali wort-koorliny

Nyit yok barnap
Baal yirra djinany
Kedalak-ngat djinda
Baal moort alitja yaakiny

Nyit yok barnap
Wadjella wangkininy
Nidja baalap nganyngany moort
Nganyang koort-ak

## Little Orphan Girl

Little orphan girl
No mother
No father
Little orphan girl

Little orphan girl
Doesn't understand
No love
Why?

White man comes
He tells orphan girl
You have no mother
No father
You won't see
Your mother and father
They have gone far away

Little orphan girl
She looks up
At the night stars
Her family are standing there

Little orphan girl
Tells the white man
Here they are, my family
In my heart

# Nyit Yok Barnap

## Little Orphan Girl

Arranged by Russell Holmes

Gina Williams and Guy Ghouse

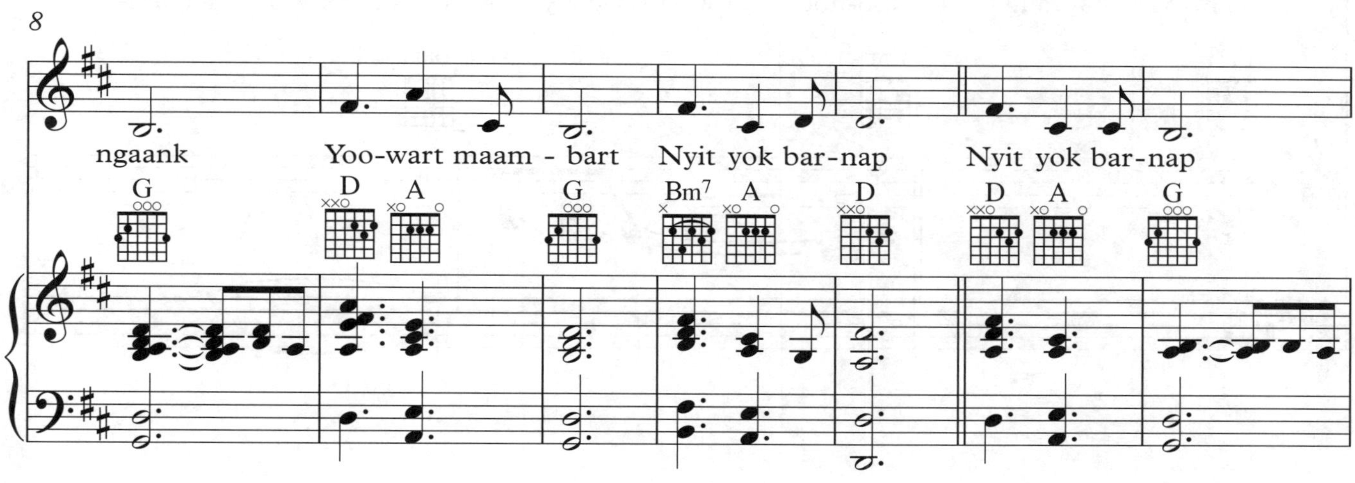


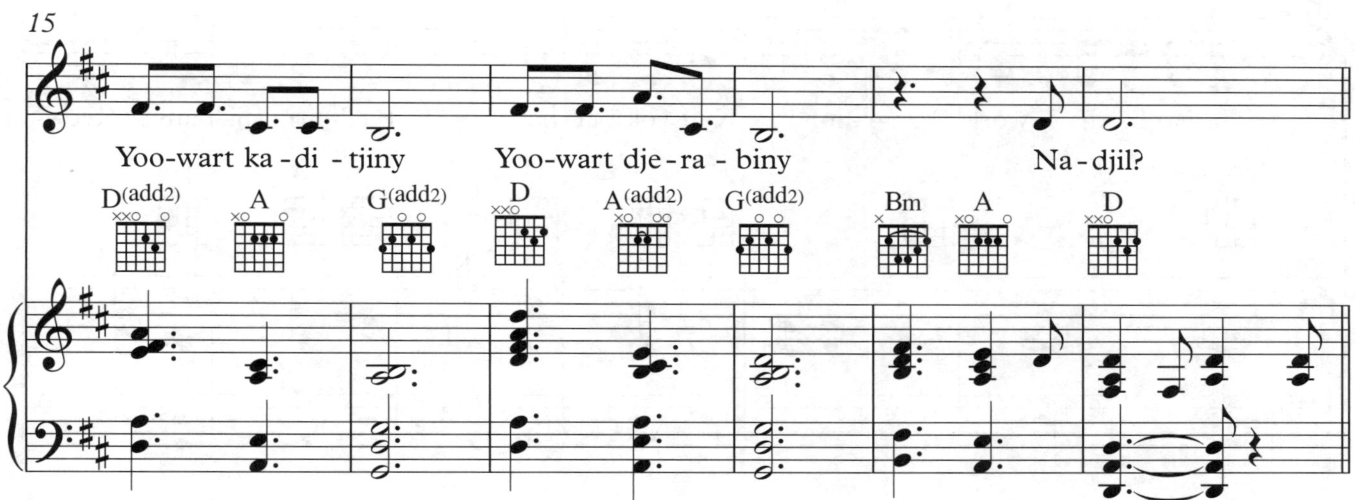

21
Wa - dje-lla koor-liny baal bar-nap yok wang-kin-iny Noo - nook yoo-wart ngaank wer
Em7
Bm7
Em7

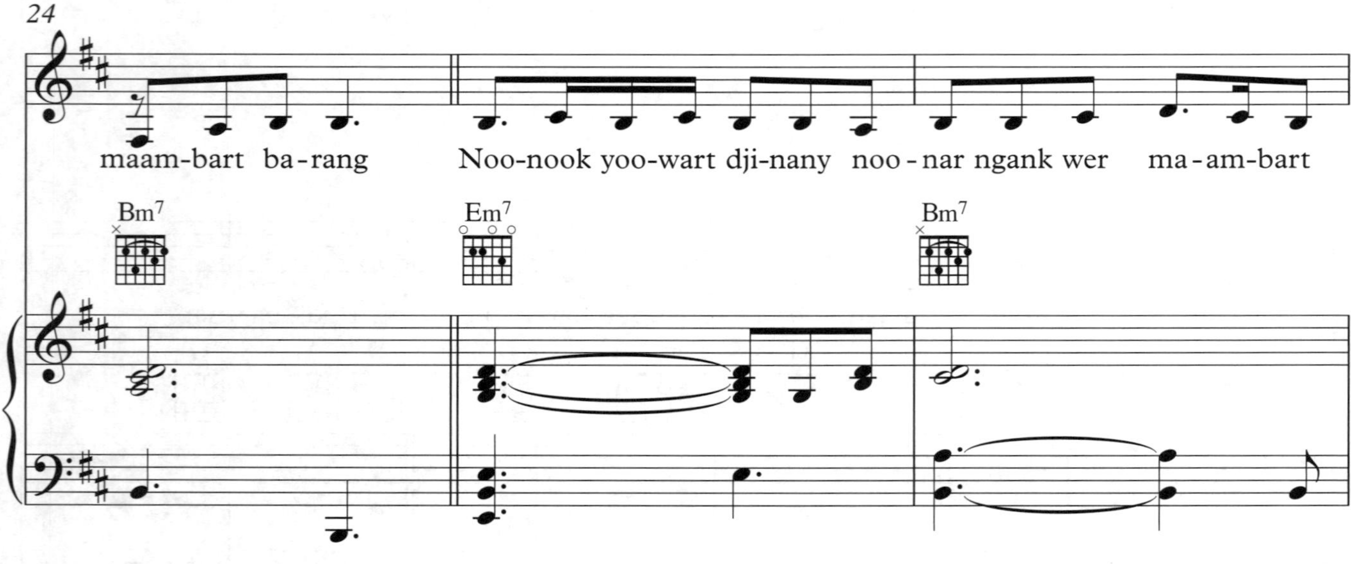
24
maam-bart ba-rang Noo-nook yoo-wart dji-nany noo - nar ngank wer ma - am-bart
Bm7
Em7
Bm7

27
Baa-lap ka-dja-li wort -koo-r-liny Nyit yok bar-nap Baal yirra dji-nany Ked-a
G(add2)
A
D
A
G
D
A
G

33
lak - ngat djin - da Baal moort a - li - tja yaa - kiny la la la
D A G(add2) Bm A(add2) D Em7

38
da da da la la la da la la la da la la la
Bm7 Em7 Bm7 Em7

42
la la la la la la la Nyit yok bar - nap Wad-je
Bm7 G A(add2) D A G

47
Rit....
lla wang - ki - niny Nid-ja baa-lap ngany-ang moort Ngany-ang ko - ort - ak
D
A
G(add2)
D
A
G(add2)
Bm
A
A7(sus4)
D

## Balladong Worl

Balladong worl yirra
Balladong worl ngany djinany
Balladong worl baalap kwobidak
Balladong worl yirra
Balladong worl ngany djinany
Warra kedala baalap wort koorliny

Djinda kanangoor baalap kwobidak
Kedala dabarkan koorliny

Balladong worl yirra
Balladong worl ngany djinany
Balladong worl baalap kwobidak
Balladong worl yirra
Balladong worl ngany djinany
Warra kedala baalap wort koorliny

Djinda karnangoor baalap kwobidak
Kedala dabarkan koorliny

Balladong worl yirra
Balladong worl ngany djinany
Warra kedala baalap wort koorliny

## Balladong Sky

Balladong skies above
Balladong skies I see
Balladong skies they are beautiful
Balladong skies above
Balladong skies I see
Bad days they go away

Stars shine they are beautiful
Days go along easily

Balladong skies above
Balladong skies I see
Balladong skies they are beautiful
Balladong skies above
Balladong skies I see
Bad days they go away

Stars shine they are beautiful
Days go along easily

Balladong skies above
Balladong skies I see
Bad days they go away

# Balladong Worl

## Balladong Sky

Arranged by Russell Holmes

Gina Williams and Guy Ghouse

Gm7
A♭maj7
B♭
B♭(sus4)
E♭
27
Ke-da-la da-bar kan koor- liny
Ball-a dong worl yi- rra
Cm7
30
- Ball - a- dong - worl ngany dji-nany -
Wa - ra ke - da-la baa-lap
A♭
E♭
Cm7
A♭maj7
32
Guitar solo till end
rit.
wort-koor - liny

## Maambart

Ngany koort moordarn
Noonook yoowart nidja
Ngany kaditjiny
Ngalak kalyakoorl

Kedalak-ngat noonook ngany djinaniny
Noonook kalyakoorl ngany koort-ak

Wer ngalak doyntj-doyntj warangka
Ngarda djinda ngalak warangka
Ngarda mikang ngalak warangka
Kalyakoorl ngalak warangka

Maambart
Ngany djinaniny, kaditjiny
Noonook wort-koorl
Ngany nidja

Kedalak-ngat noonook ngany djinaniny
Noonook kalyakoorl ngany koort-ak

Wer ngalak doyntj-doyntj warangka
Ngarda djinda ngalak warangka
Ngarda mikang ngalak warangka
Kalyakoorl ngalak warangka

Kedalak-ngat noonook ngany djinaniny
Noonook kalyakoorl ngany koort-ak

Wer ngalak doyntj-doyntj warangka
Ngarda djinda ngalak warangka
Ngarda mikang ngalak warangka
Kalyakoorl ngalak warangka

## Father

My heart it is heavy
You are not here
I thought
We would be forever

Every night I see you
You're forever in my heart

And together we sing
Under stars, we sing
Under moonlight, we sing
Forever we sing

Father
I see and understand
You are gone
I am here

Every night I see you
You're forever in my heart

And together we sing
Under stars, we sing
Under moonlight, we sing
Forever we sing

Every night I see you
You're forever in my heart

And together we sing
Under stars, we sing
Under moonlight, we sing
Forever we sing

# Maambart
## Father

Arranged by Russell Holmes

Gina Williams and Guy Ghouse

D C Em
43
Noo-nook wort-koorl, Ngany ni - dja Ked-a-lak- ngat
D Em A A(sus4)
48
noo-nook ngany dji-na-niny Noo-nook ka - lya-koorl, ngany koort - ak
A D C D
54
Wer nga - lak doy-ntj doyntj wa- rang - ka Nga-rda dji - nda
C D/C C D C C/D C
60
nga-lak wa-rang - ka Nga-rda mi-kang nga-lak wa-rang - ka
Fmaj7 A(add2) D D7(sus4) D D C
67
Ka - lya-koorl nga-lak wa-rang - ka La - da da da da da da da - da
D C
74
da - da da dah - - - da da da da
Fmaj7 A7(sus4) A7(♭9) D(sus4) D
78
da

## Ngany Koorliny

Ngany moordang-ngat koorliny
Dalanginy nganyang koort dook-nginy
Yoowart kaditj windji ngany koorliny
Ngany kaditjiny ngany wort-koorliny

Ngany nidja wer ngany kaditjiny
Dalanginy nganyang koorndarm
Ngany yoowart kweyiny yeyi
Yirra Maaman ngany djinaniny

Ngany yirra yaakiny wer ngany koorliny
Ngany djaliny nganyang koort dook-nginy
Wer ngany djinaniny moonboorli
Koora koora ngany kweyiny

Ngany yirra yaakiny wer ngany koorliny
Ngany djarliny nganyang koort dook-nginy
Wer ngany djinaniny moornboorli
Koora koora ngany kweyiny

Keyen kedala ngany yoowart nidja
Ngany yoowarl-koorl ngarda boodjar-ak
Ngany yoowart kweyiny yeyi
Yirra Maaman ngany djinaniny
Yirra Maaman ngany djinaniny

## I'm Going

I moved in the dark places
Following my heartbeat
No idea where I'm going
But I know I'm on my way

I am here and I am learning
I am following my dream
I am not afraid now
My Creator is watching me

I'm standing up and I'm going
I'm listening to my heartbeat
And I'm looking beyond
What frightened me in the past

I'm standing up and I'm going
I'm listening to my heartbeat
And I'm looking beyond
What frightened me in the past

One day I won't be here
I'll go back down to the earth
I'm not afraid now
My Creator is watching me
My Creator is watching me

# Ngany Koorliny

## I'm Going

Arranged by Russell Holmes

Guy Ghouse and Gina Williams

Guitar Intro

♩ = 80

Am(add9) C D Am(add9)

Ngany moor-dang-ngat
Ngany ni - dja wer

C D Am(add9) C

— koor - liny — Dal - an - giny ngany- ang — koort
ngany ka — di - tjiny — Dal - an - giny ngany - ang — koo-

D Am(add9) C D

— dook nginy — Yoo-wart ka ditj wind — ji ngany koor liny —
- rn - darm — Ngany yoo-wart kweyiny — yeyi

1. 2.

F G Am(add9) Fmaj7 G

— Ngany ka-di - tjiny — ngany wort - koo - liny —
Yi-rra Maa — man ngany dji-na- niny —

Am(add9) Bm7 G

Ngany yi - rra yaa-kin wer ngany ko-or- liny —

Bm7 G B♭ C

Ngany dja - liny ngany-ang koort doo - k- nginy — Wer ngany djin-a- niny

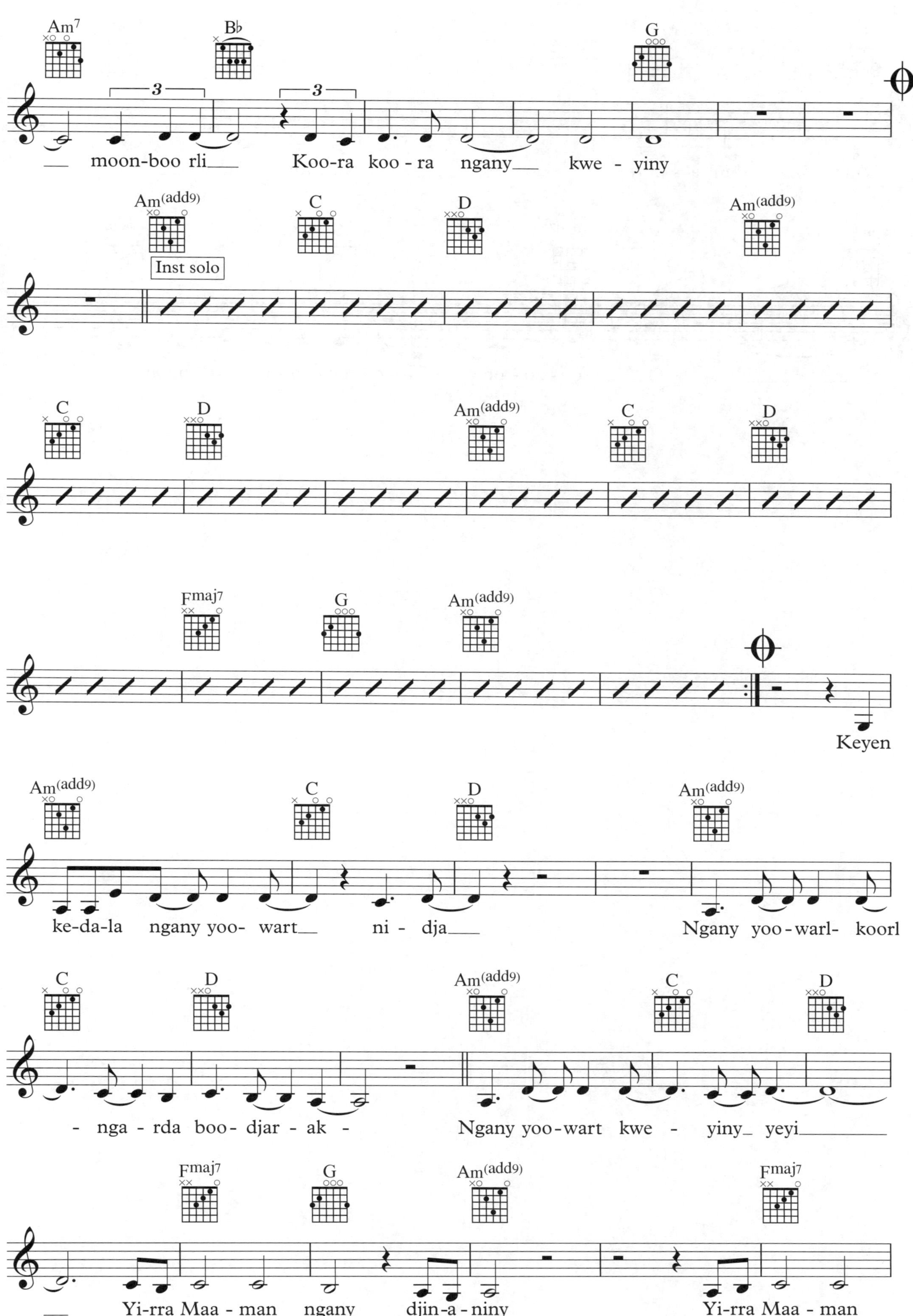

Am7
B♭
G
moon-boo rli Koo-ra koo-ra ngany kwe - yiny
Am(add9)
C
D
Am(add9)
Inst solo
C
D
Am(add9)
C
D
Fmaj7
G
Am(add9)
Keyen
Am(add9)
C
D
Am(add9)
ke-da-la ngany yoo- wart ni - dja Ngany yoo-warl- koorl
C
D
Am(add9)
C
D
- nga - rda boo- djar - ak - Ngany yoo-wart kwe - yiny yeyi
Fmaj7
G
Am(add9)
Fmaj7
Yi-rra Maa - man ngany djin-a-niny Yi-rra Maa - man

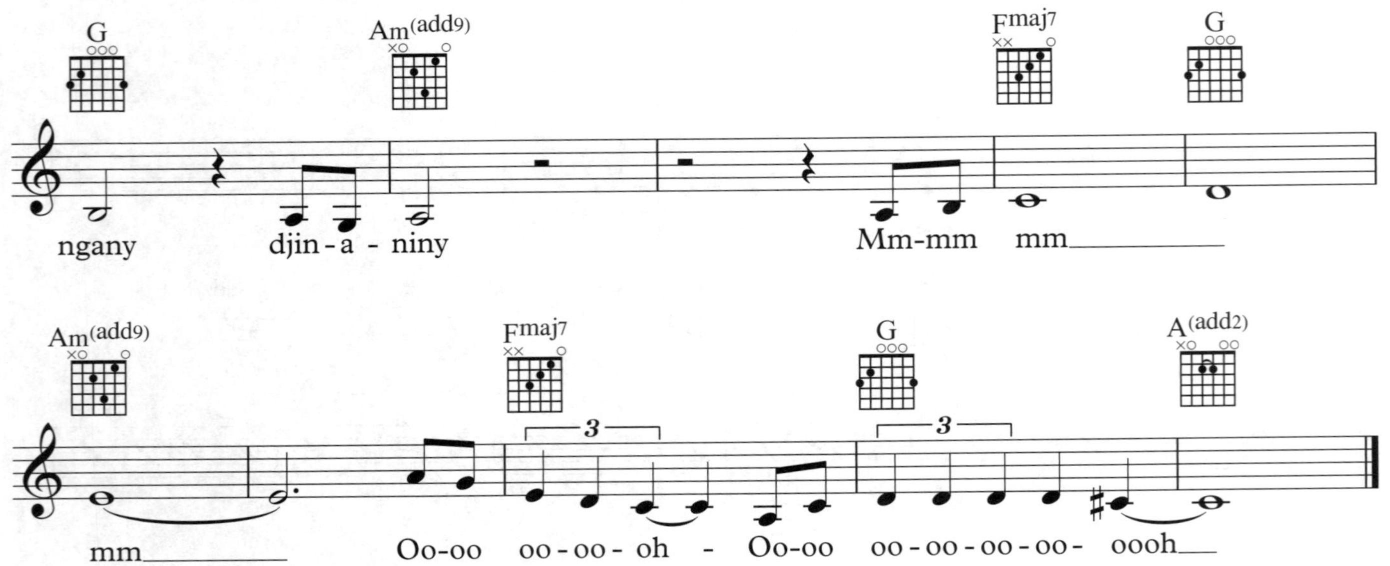
G
Am(add9)
Fmaj7
G
ngany djin - a - niny
Mm-mm mm
Am(add9)
Fmaj7
G
A(add2)
3
3
mm
Oo-oo oo - oo - oh - Oo-oo oo - oo - oo - oo- oooh

## Moordiyap

Moordiyap, moordiyap
Aliwah nop wort djakoorliny
Moordiyap, moordiyap
Wadjella yoowarl-koorliny
Moordiyap, moordiyap
Aliwah nop wort djakoorliny
Moordiyap, moordiyap
Wadjella yoowarl-koorliny

Ngaank koort baal dabarkan djakaroony
Boodja-k balyan baal miyaldjan
Nganyang maambart yoowart kaaditj
Ngany wort-koorliny

Moordiyap, moordiyap
Aliwah nop wort djakoorliny
Moordiyap, moordiyap
Wadjella yoowarl-koorliny

Nganyang boodja baal naatj ngany koordak
Kwobidak koortaboodja
Nganyang moort baalap alitja
Baalap yelakitj

Moordiyap, moordiyap
Aliwah nop wort djakoorliny
Moordiyap, moordiyap
Wadjella yoowarl-koorliny

## Hurry Up

Hurry up, hurry up
Look out boy, run away
Hurry up, hurry up
White man is coming
Hurry up, hurry up
Look out boy, run away
Hurry up, hurry up
White man is coming

Mother's heart slowly breaks
Land is wet with her tears
My father doesn't know
I am gone

Hurry up, hurry up
Look out boy, run away
Hurry up, hurry up
White man is coming

My land is what I long for
Beautiful heartland
My family, they are there
They wait

Hurry up, hurry up
Look out boy, run away
Hurry up, hurry up
White man is coming

# Moordiyap

## Hurry Up

Arranged by Russell Holmes

Gina Williams and Guy Ghouse

Em F♯m7 Am F G Em F♯m7
34
koor-liny Moor di - yap, moor di-yap Wa-dje-lla yoo-warl-koor - liny
D Am
39
Ngany-ang boo - dja baal - naatj_ngany-ko - or - dak_
D Am D
43
Kwo-bi-da - k koorta_ bo - o- dja_ Ngan-yang mo - ort baa
Am E7
48
- lap_ a - li - tja_ baa-lap ye - la-kitj_
Am F G Em F♯m7
53
Moor di - yap, moor di - yap A - li-wah nop wort dja koor-liny
Am F G Em F♯m7
57
Moor di - yap, moor di - yap Wa-dje-lla yoo-warl - koorliny
Am
61
Riff
1.
2.

## Iggy's Lullaby

Nookert ngoorndiny ngany kwop koorlangka
Kedalak djinda kanangoor
Kedala wort koorl
Benang yoowarl koorl
Nookert maawit nookert

Nookert ngoorndiny ngany kwop koorlangka
Kedalak djinda kanangoor
Kedala wort koorl
Benang yoowarl koorl
Nookert maawit nookert

Lay down to sleep my beautiful child
Stars shine in the sky
Today's gone but
Tomorrow's coming

Nookert ngoorndiny ngany kwop koorlangka
Kedalak djinda kanangoor
Kedala wort koorl
Benang yoowarl koorl
Nookert maawit nookert
Kaya

# Iggy's Lullaby

F C G G C F C
37
DS al coda
sky To-day's gone but to- morr-ow's
G C F C F C
43
co- ming Noo-kert ngoorn-diny ngany kwopkoor-lang-ka Ke-da-lak dji-n-da
p
Am G F C F C
48
ka - nan-goor Ke - da-la wort-koorl, be-nang yoowarl - koorl
F C G G C Cmaj7 F
51
p
4X
fine
Noo-kert ma-a-wit noo-kert Ka - ya

## Boorda

Kwobidak koorda
Ngalak yoowart boorda-wangk
Ngalang koort baalap moordarn
Noonook wort-koorliny bokadja

Ngalak kanyiny ngarla-karla naariny
Keyen kedala noonook yoowarl koorl
Ngalak djerabiny alitja kedala
Noonook yoowarl koorl
Noonook yoowarl koorl

Boorda, boorda
Noonook moorditj koorliny
Boorda
Boorda, boorda
Ngalak djinany noonook
Boorda

Ngalak kanyiny ngarla-karla naariny
Keyen kedala noonook yoowarl koorl
Ngalak djerabiny alitja kedala
Noonook yoowarl koorl
Noonook yoowarl koorl

Boorda, boorda
Noonook moorditj koorliny,
Boorda
Boorda, boorda
Ngalak djinany noonook
Boorda

## Soon (By and By)

Beautiful friends
We don't want to say goodbye
Our hearts are sorry
You're going far away

We'll keep the home fires burning
One day you'll return
We'll look forward to that day
You come home
You come home

By and by, by and by
May you have strong/solid travels
By and by
By and by, by and by
We'll see you
By and by

We'll keep the home fires burning
One day you'll return
We'll look forward to that day
You come home
You come home

By and by, by and by
May you have strong/solid travels
By and by
By and by, by and by
We'll see you
By and by

# Boorda

## Soon (By and By)

Fmaj7 E7 Am7 Dm7 Am7 Dm7
27
Nga-lak djin-any noonook Boo r - da
F(add2) C F(add2) C
3fr
33
Nga-lak kan-yiny ngar-la-kar-la na -a-riny Keyen ke-da-la-noo-nook yoo- warl_ ko-o-rl
Dm Am Dm
37
Nga-lak djera-biny al-itja ke-da-la____ Noo-nook yoo-warl-koorl
G Dm7 Am7 Dm7
40
noo-nook yoo-warl-koorl Boor - da____bo-or-da Noo-nook moor-ditj koor- liny_boo-r
Am7 Dm7 Am7 Fmaj7 E7
44
da Boor - da____bo-or da Nga-lak djin-any noo nook-Bo-o-rda
Am Dm Am Dm Am Dm
49
Oo-oo-oo-oo-ooh Oo-oo-oo-oo-ooh Oo____oo-oo ooh
Am Dm Fmaj7 E7
55
Oo________oo-oo-ooh Nga-lak djin-any noo-nook Bo-or - da

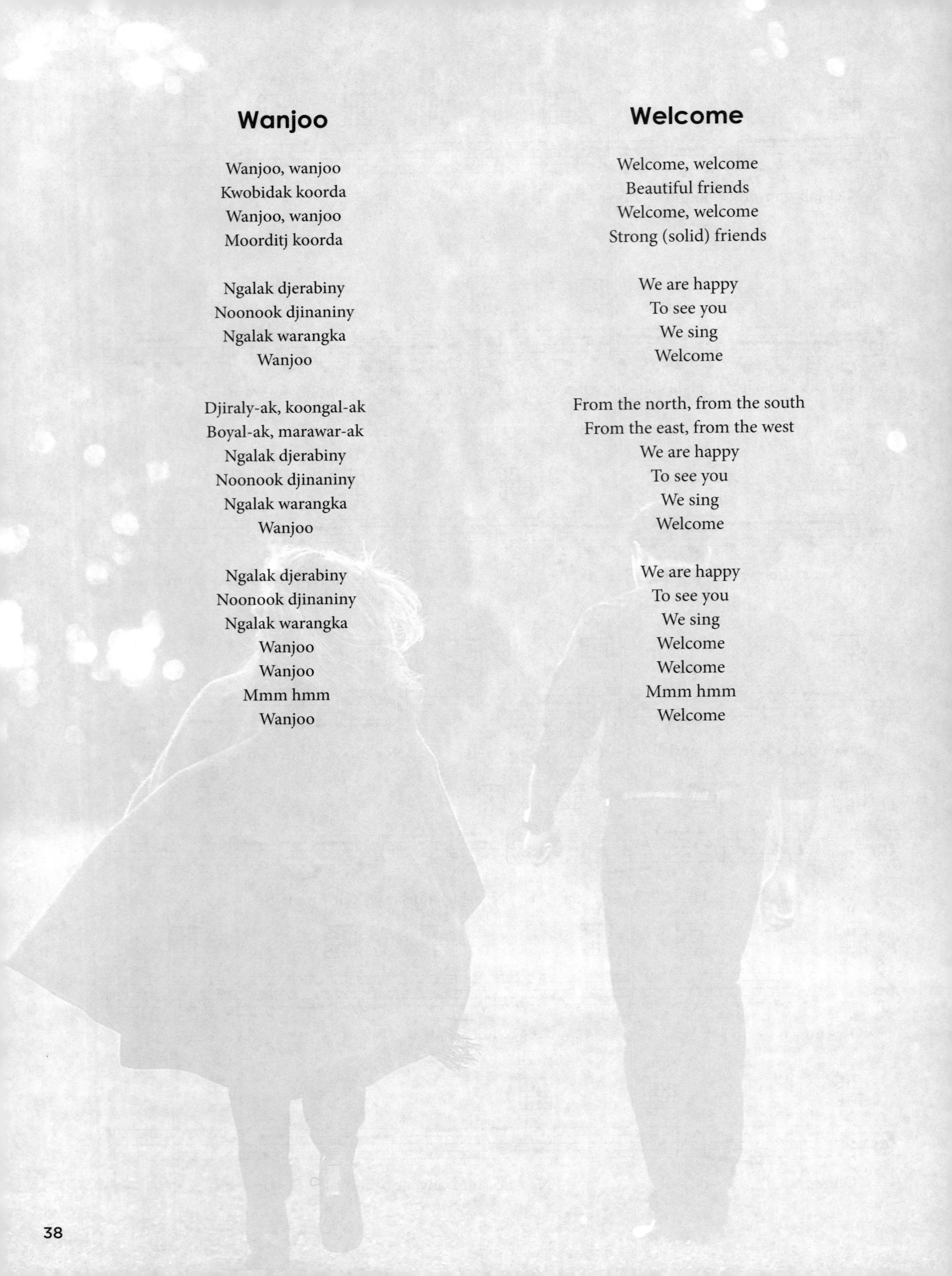

## Wanjoo

Wanjoo, wanjoo
Kwobidak koorda
Wanjoo, wanjoo
Moorditj koorda

Ngalak djerabiny
Noonook djinaniny
Ngalak warangka
Wanjoo

Djiraly-ak, koongal-ak
Boyal-ak, marawar-ak
Ngalak djerabiny
Noonook djinaniny
Ngalak warangka
Wanjoo

Ngalak djerabiny
Noonook djinaniny
Ngalak warangka
Wanjoo
Wanjoo
Mmm hmm
Wanjoo

## Welcome

Welcome, welcome
Beautiful friends
Welcome, welcome
Strong (solid) friends

We are happy
To see you
We sing
Welcome

From the north, from the south
From the east, from the west
We are happy
To see you
We sing
Welcome

We are happy
To see you
We sing
Welcome
Welcome
Mmm hmm
Welcome

# Wanjoo

## Welcome

Arranged by Russell Holmes

Gina Williams and Guy Ghouse

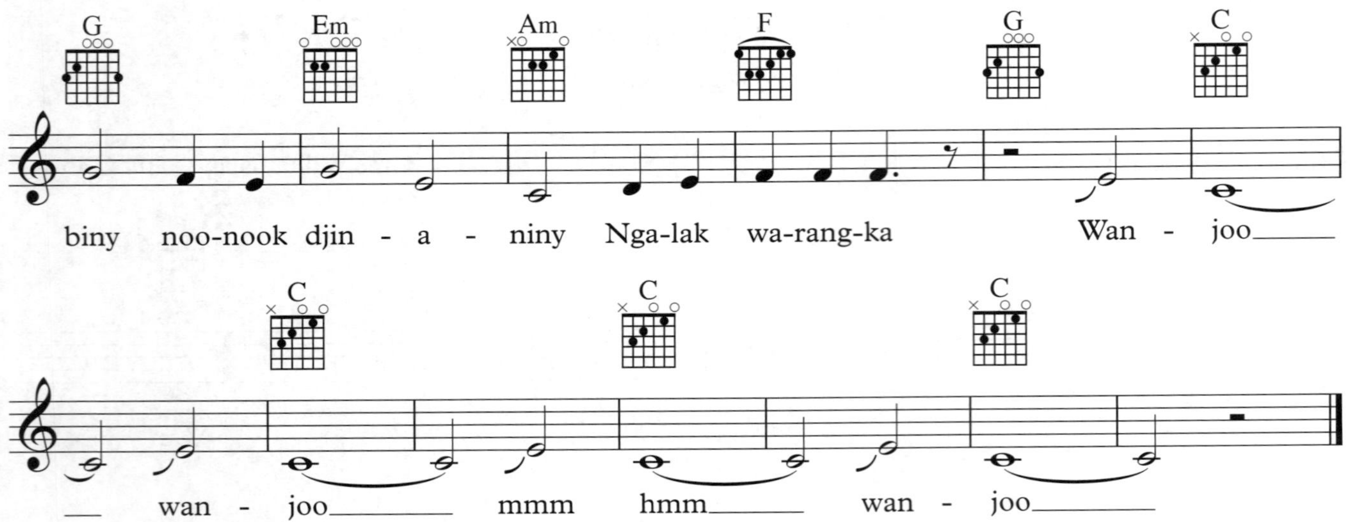
G
Em
Am
F
G
C
biny noo-nook djin - a - niny Nga-lak wa-rang-ka Wan - joo
C
C
C
wan - joo mmm hmm wan - joo

BINDI
Gina Williams & Guy

## Ngalak Yoowart Waahliny

Ngalak yoowart waahliny
Ngalak keyen danjoo yirra yaakiny
Moorditj koorliny, boodjar-ak koorliny
Ngalak yoowart waahliny
Ngalak yoowart waahliny

Noonar wangkiny yoowart baakan
Ngalang moortung nidja wer ngalak moorditj
Mininy kep-koorliny ngalak kakarook
Wer malkar baal koorliny, ngalak warangka

Ngalak yoowart waahliny
Ngalak keyen danjoo yirra yaakiny
Moorditj koorliny, boodjar-ak koorliny
Ngalak yoowart waahliny
Ngalak yoowart waahliny

Noonook kwilya, wangkiny baal marr-mokiny
Ngalak karnant wangkiny
Ngalang koort-ak baalap kanyiny
Mininy kep-koorliny ngalak kakarook
Wer malkar baal koorliny ngalak warangka

Ngalak yoowart waahliny
Ngalak yoowart waahliny
Ngalak yoowart waahliny

Noonook kwilya, wangkiny baal marr-mokiny
Ngalak karnant wangkiny
Ngalang koort-ak baalap kanyiny
Mininy kep-koorliny ngalak kakarook
Wer malkar baal koorliny ngalak warangka

Ngalak yoowart waahliny
Ngalak keyen danjoo yirra yaakiny
Moorditj koorliny, boodjar-ak koorliny
Ngalak yoowart waahliny
Ngalak yoowart waahliny

Ngalak yoowart waahliny
Ngalak yoowart waahliny

## We Won't Cry

We won't cry
We're standing up together as one
Moving strong, on this land, moving
We won't cry
We won't cry

Your words won't hurt
Our people are here, and we're strong
If rains come we'll dance
And storms they come, we'll sing

We won't cry
We're standing up together as one
Moving strong, on this land, moving
We won't cry
We won't cry

You lie, words are like a wind cloud
We speak the truth,
We keep it in our hearts
If rains come we'll dance
And storms they come we'll sing

We won't cry
We won't cry
We won't cry

You lie, words are like a wind cloud
We speak the truth
We keep it in our hearts
If rains come we'll dance
And storms they come we'll sing

We won't cry
We're standing up together as one
Moving strong, on this land, moving
We won't cry
We won't cry

We won't cry
We won't cry

# Ngalak Yoowart Waahliny

## We Won't Cry

Arranged by Russell Holmes

Gina Williams and Guy Ghouse

1.
2.
Em Am7 C D C D Bm7(sus4)
26
yoo-waart waah-liny Nga-lak Noo-nook kw-il ya,
D/A G6/9 F♯m7
30
wang -kiny ba-al marr-mo-kiny Nga-lak kar-nant wang- kiny,nga-lang koort-ak baa-lap kan-yiny
Bm7(sus4) D/A C
33
Mi-ni -ny kep - koor-liny nga-lak ka-ka-rook W-er mal-kar baal koor-liny nga-lak
D Em Bm7(sus4)
repeat 8x
36
wa-rang-ka Nga-lak yoo-wart waah-liny Nga-lak Noo-nook kw-il ya,
A/D G6/9 F♯m7
40
wang -kiny ba-al marr-mo-kiny Nga-lak kar-nant wang- kiny,nga-lang koort-ak baa-lap kan-yiny
Bm7(sus4) A/D C
43
Mi-ni -ny kep - koor-liny nga-lak ka-ka-rook W-er mal-kar baal koor-liny nga-lak
D Em Am7 C D
46
wa-rang-ka Nga-lak yoo-wart waah-liny Nga-lak ke-yen dan-joo yir-ra yaa-kiny
Em Am7 C D Em Am7
49
Moor-ditj koor-liny, boo-djar - ak koor-liny Nga-lak yoo-wart waah-liny

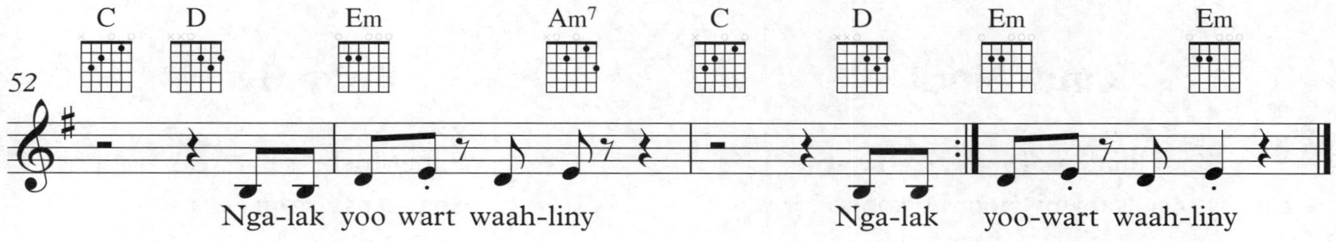
C
D
Em
Am7
C
D
Em
Em
52
Nga-lak yoo wart waah-liny
Nga-lak yoo-wart waah-liny

## Bindi Bindi

Bindi Bindi baal yoowart winyarn
Baal kanyiny moorditj koort
Bindi Bindi baal djerabiny
Baal yoowart koordak naatj yoowart baal

Bindi Bindi baal kwobidak
Baal yoowart koora kweyiny
Bindi Bindi baal moorditj
Baal mila-ngat djinaniny

Kwobidak, kalyakoorl
Kwobidak, kalyakoorl

Bindi Bindi baal kakarook
Djinany baal wort-koorliny
Bindi Bindi baal warangka
Boorda wangkininy

Kwobidak, kalyakoorl
Kwobidak, kalyakoorl

Bindi Bindi baal yoowart winyarn
Baal kanyiny moorditj koort
Bindi Bindi baal djerabiny
Baal yoowart koordak naatj yoowart baal

Kalyakoorl
Kwobidak, kalyakoorl

Kwobidak, kalyakoorl
Kwobidak, kalyakoorl

## Butterfly

Butterfly she is not weak
She keeps a strong heart
Butterfly is happy
She doesn't yearn for what is not hers

Butterfly she is beautiful
She's not afraid of her past
Butterfly she is strong
She's looking to her future

Beautiful, forever
Beautiful, forever

Butterfly she is dancing
Watch her leaving
Butterfly she is singing
Talk to you soon

Beautiful, forever
Beautiful, forever

Butterfly she is not weak
She keeps a strong heart
Butterfly is happy
She doesn't yearn for what is not hers

Forever
Beautiful, forever

Beautiful, forever
Beautiful, forever

# Bindi Bindi

## Butterfly

F(add9) Am C G Am G C F G
34
Bin-di Bin-di ba-al ka-ka-rook Dji-nany ba-al wort - koor-liny
Am C G Am G C F G Am
39
Bin-di Bin-di ba-al war-ang-ka Boor-da wang-ki-ni ny Kwo-bi-dak
Dm7 C/E F G Am Am/G F G
44
kal-ya-koorl Kwo-bi-dak
Dm7 C/E F(add9) Am C G Am
49
Hits
kal-ya-koorl Bin-di Bin-di ba-al yoo-wart win-yarn
G C F G Am C G Am
53
Baal kan-yiny mo-or - ditj koort Bin-di Bin-di ba-al dje-ra-biny
G C F G Am Am/G
57
Baal yoo-wart koor-dak - naatj yoo-wart baal
Dm7 C/E F G Am Am/G F G Dm7 C/E F(add9)
60
Kal-ya-koorl Kwo bi dak, kal-ya-koorl

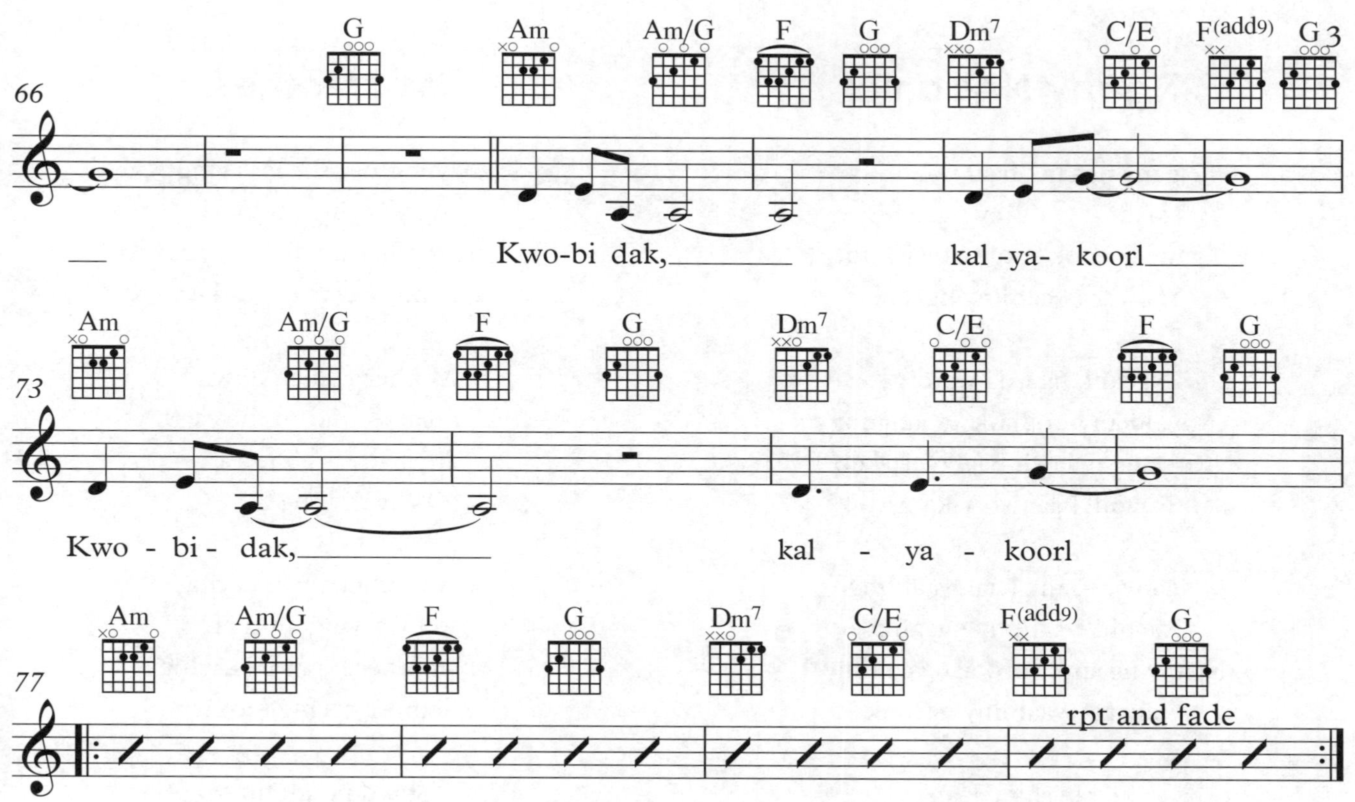
G Am Am/G F G Dm7 C/E F(add9) G 3
66
Kwo-bi dak, kal -ya- koorl
Am Am/G F G Dm7 C/E F G
73
Kwo - bi - dak, kal - ya - koorl
Am Am/G F G Dm7 C/E F(add9) G
77
rpt and fade

## Ngany Ngaank

Ngany ngaank baal waahliny
Naadjil waahliny ngaank?
Ngany ngaank yoowart waahliny
Yoowart waahliny ngaank

Ngaank ngarda werdiny
Miyaldjan boodja-k kanangoor
Nganyang maawit baal wort-koorl
Naadjil baal wort-koorl?

Ngany ngaank baal waahliny
Naadjil waahliny ngaank?
Ngany ngaank yoowart waahliny
Yoowart waahliny ngaank

Yirra yaak ngaank
Yoowart waahliny nganyang ngaank
Moorditj koorliny boodjar-ak
Maawit yoowarl-koorl

Ngany ngaank baal waahliny
Naadjil waahliny ngaank?
Ngany ngaank yoowart waahliny
Yoowart waahliny ngaank

## My Mother

My mother she is crying
Why crying mother?
My mother no more crying
No more crying mother

Mother's fallen down
Her tears shine on the earth
"My baby is gone away
Why did she go?"

My mother she is crying
Why crying mother?
My mother no more crying
No more crying mother

Stand up mother
No more crying my mother
Walk strong on our land
Your baby, she returns

My mother she is crying
Why crying mother?
My mother no more crying
No more crying mother

# Ngany Ngaank
## My Mother

Arranged by Russell Holmes

Gina Williams and Guy Ghouse

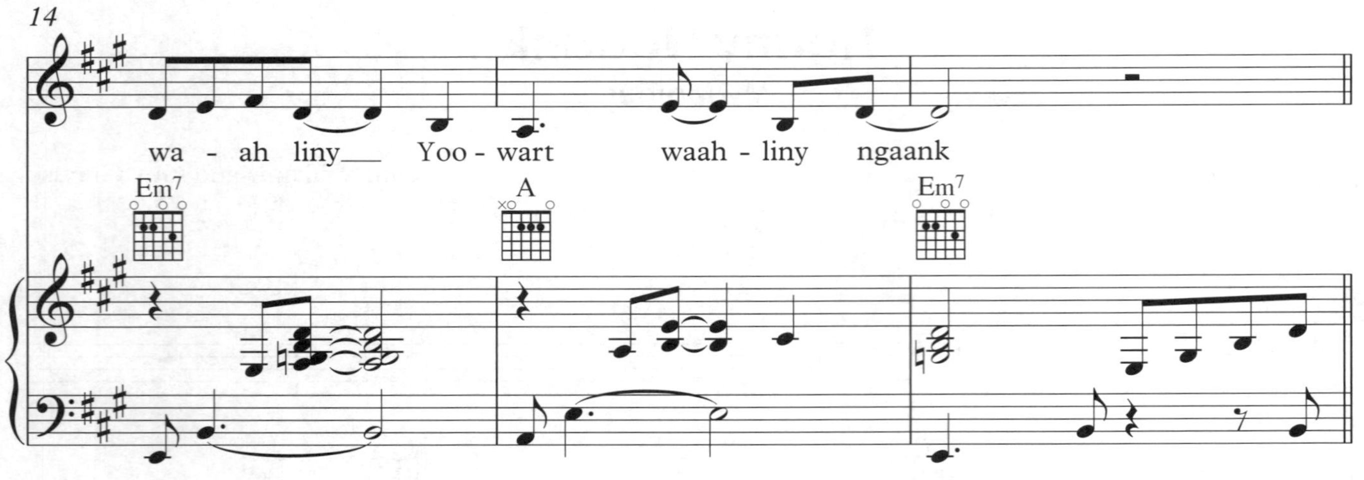
14
wa - ah liny Yoo - wart waah - liny ngaank
Em7
A
Em7

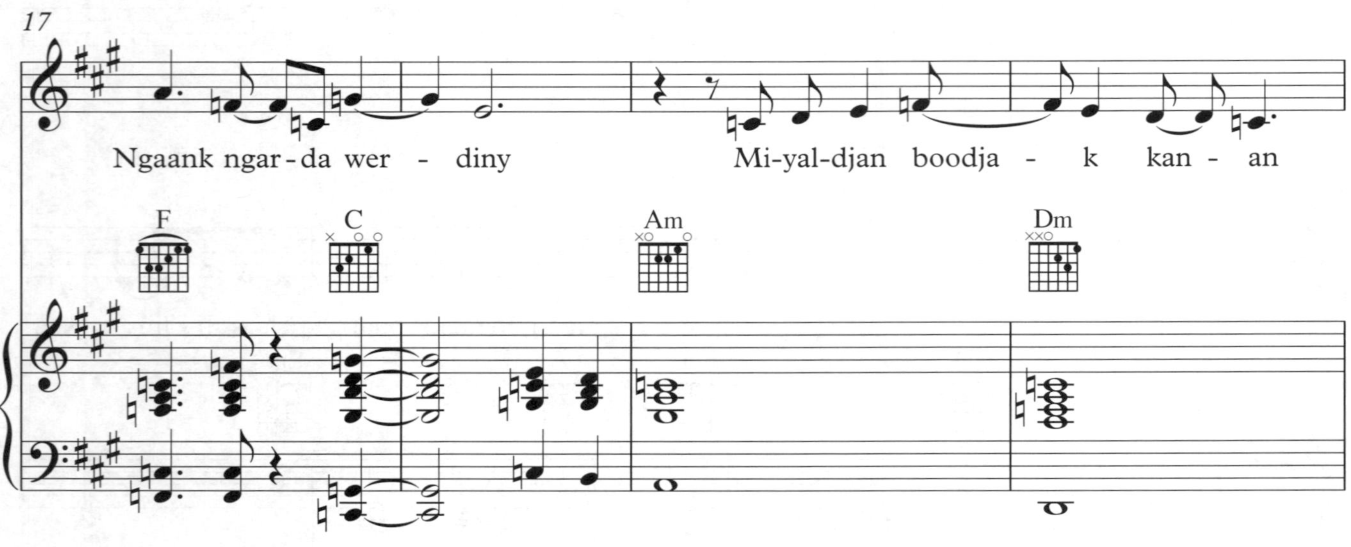
17
Ngaank ngar - da wer - diny Mi - yal - djan boodja - k kan - an
F
C
Am
Dm

21
goor Ngan - yang maa - wit baal - wort - koorl
Am
F

24
Naa - djil baal wort- koorl?
Ngany ngaank baal
C
G
A

28
wa - ah liny Naa - djil waah - liny ngaank?
Em7
A
Em7

31
Ngany ngaank yoo - wart wa - ah liny Yoo - wart waah-liny ngaank
A
Em7
A
Em7

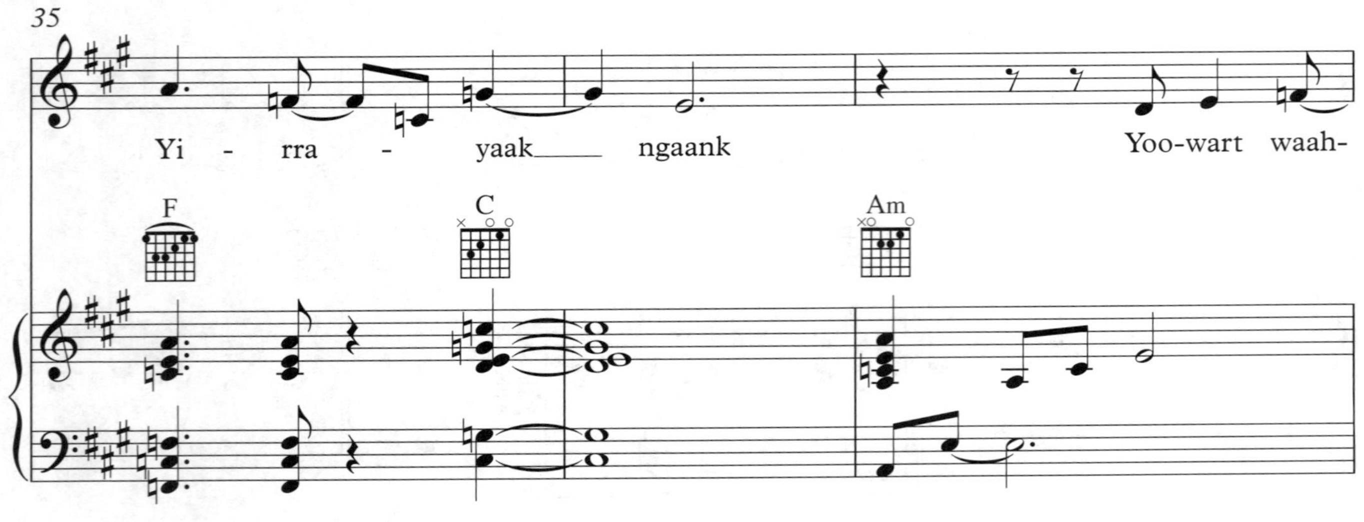

35
Yi - rra - yaak ngaank Yoo-wart waah-
F
C
Am


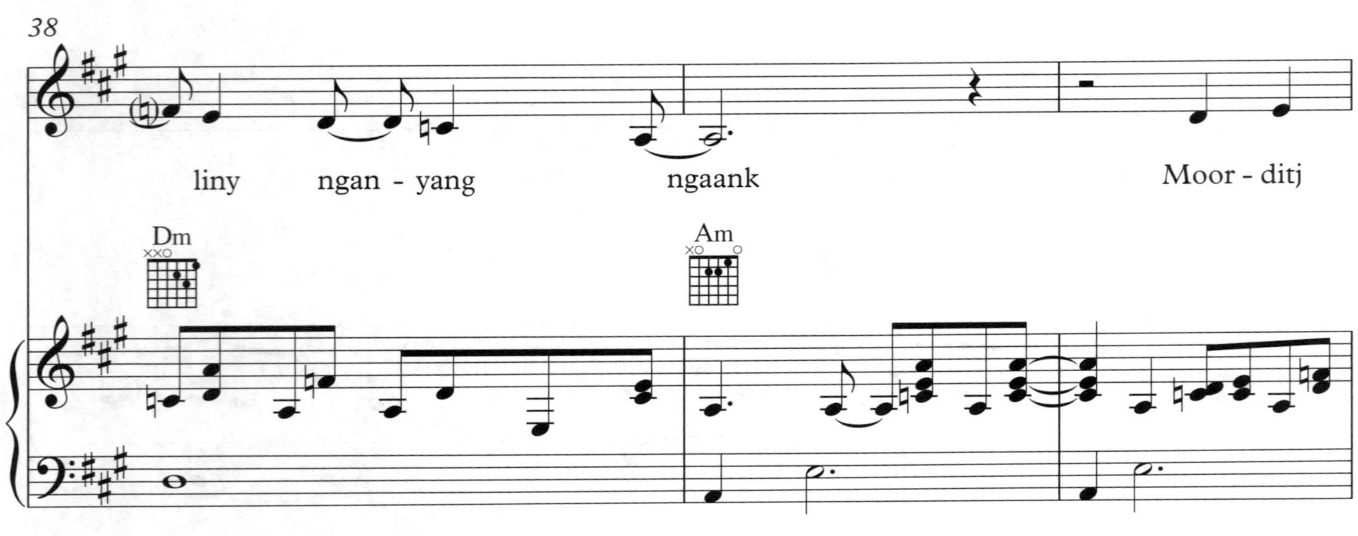

38
liny ngan - yang ngaank Moor - ditj
Dm
Am

41
koor-liny boo - djar - ak Ma-a-wit yoowarl- koorl
Dm
C
G
G
E/G♯

45
Ngany ngaank baal wa - ah-liny Naa - djil waah - liny ngaank?
A
Em7
A

48
Ngany ngaank yooo - wart waah - liny Yoo- wart
Em7
A
Em7

51
waah - liny ngaank Na
A
Em7
A

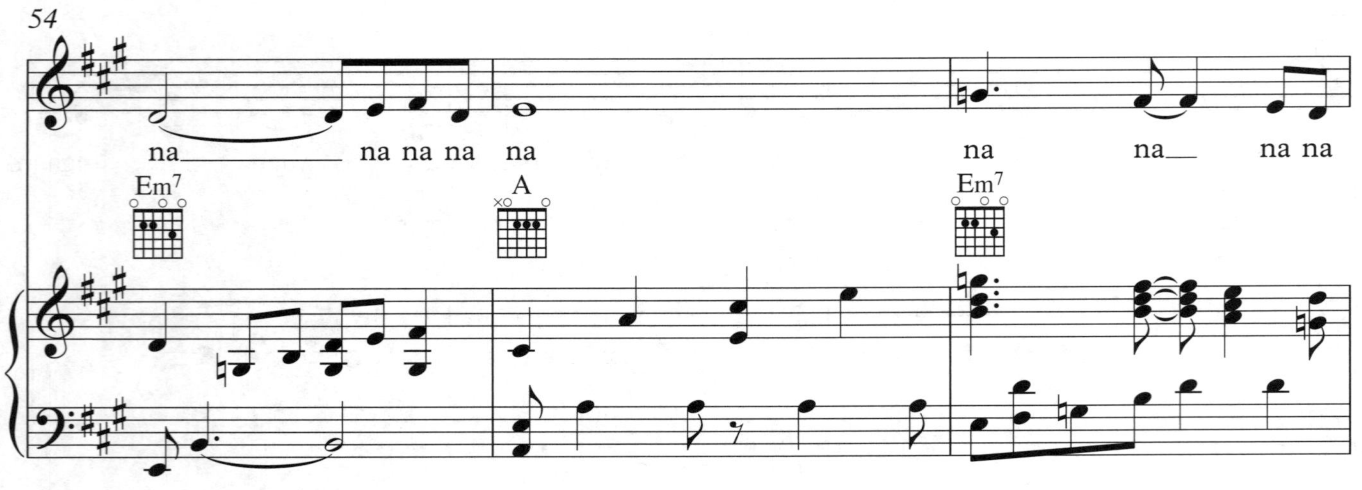
54
na na na na na na na na na na
Em7
A
Em7

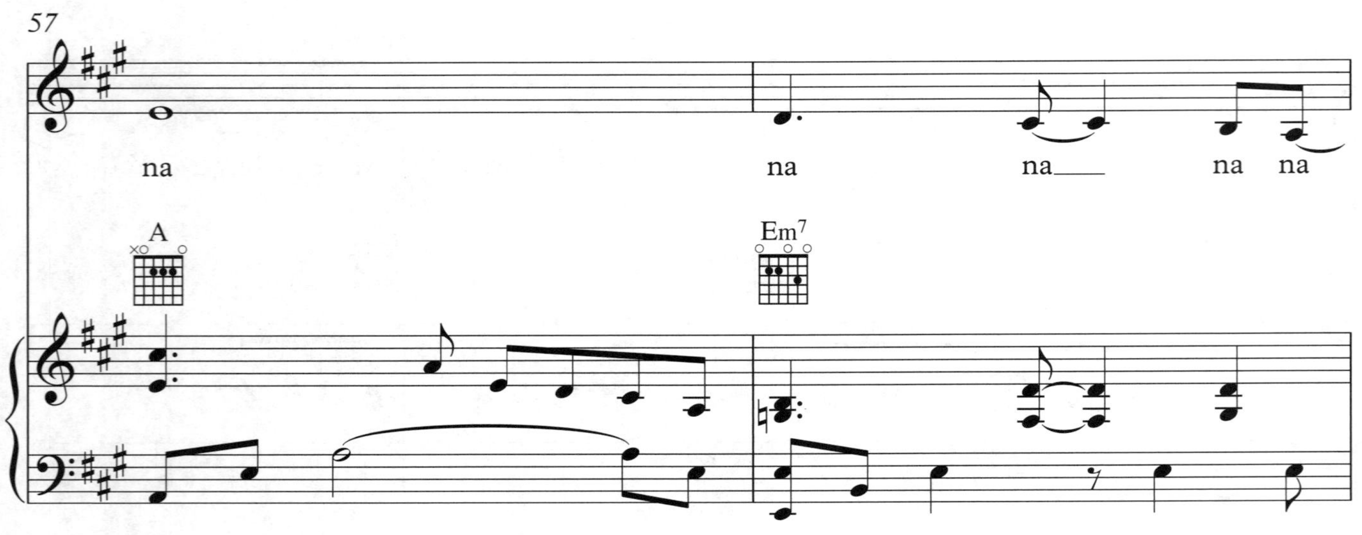
57
na na na na na
A
Em7

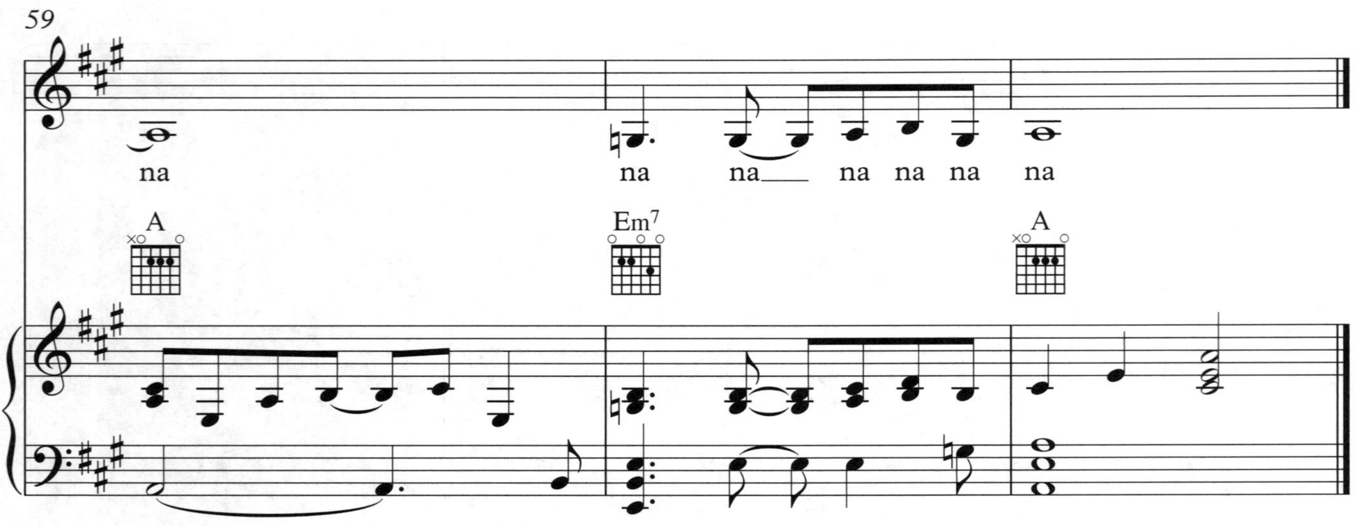
59
na na na na na na na
A
Em7
A

## Ninnyok

Ninnyok, Ninnyok
Yirra yaakiny Ninnyok
Dabakarn koorliny
Noonar *Kongk baal koorliny
Noonook yoowart kweyiny yeyi
Ngalak wanjoo warangka
Noonook djinany noonar Kongk
Baal bardook, baal yelakitj

Little Girl, Little Girl
Stand tall Little Girl
Go along steadily
*He is there, he's travelling
Don't you be frightened now
We will sing a welcome song
You will see him very soon
He's close, he is waiting

*Kongk = Uncle

# Ninnyok

## Little Girl

Arranged by Russell Holmes

Gina Williams and Guy Ghouse

53
C
F/C
Gm7
there, he's tra - ve- ling Don't you be frigh-tened now We will sing a
61
C7
F
Fm
C
G
wel-come song You will see him ve - ry soon He's close he is wa - i -
70
C
G
C
G
G7
C
repeat ad lib till Cue
ting Nin - ny - Nin - ny- ok
76
G7
C
G7
C
G7
C
Nin - ny- ok Nin - ny- ok Nin - ny- ok

## Koorlbardi wer Wardong

Koora nyittiny boodja
Koorlbardi wer Wardong
Moorditj koorda, baalap koorda kalyakoorl
Warra kedala yoowarl-koorl
Warra kedala kwop koorda
Warra kedala yoowarl-koorl
Yoowart moorditj koorda!

Bilya-k, Koorlbardi
Barna baal wangkininy
Nyin baal kwobidak? Nyin baal kwobidak?
Barna doyntj-doyntj wangkininy
Noonook BOOLA kwobidak
Wardong baal djinaniny
Koorlbardi aliwah!

Wardong, Koorlbardi
Baalap koomba bakadjoo
Ngarda werdiny karla-k
Baalap yoowart kwobidak
Warra kedala nidja
Koora moorditj koorda
Barna wangkiny dima
Aliwah! Aliwah!

## Magpie and Crow

Long ago cold earth (creation)
Magpie and Crow
Solid friends, they were friends forever
Bad days coming
Bad days, good friends
Bad days coming
Not solid friends!

At the river, Magpie
Talking to the animals
Who's the prettiest? Who's the prettiest?
Animals join together to say
You're VERY beautiful
Crow is watching
Look out Magpie!

Crow, Magpie
They have a big fight
Fall down into the fire
They're not beautiful
Bad days are here
For old, good friends
Animals all shout
Look out! Look out!

# Koorlbardi wer Wardong

## Magpie and Crow

Arranged by Russell Holmes

Gina Williams and Guy Ghouse

Instrumental Harmonica melody

140 bpm

E♭ B♭(add2)/D Cm7 A♭maj7 B♭ Cm7 E♭ B♭(add2)/D Cm7 A♭maj7 B♭

8
Cm7 Cm7 Gm7 Cm7

Koo-ra nyit-tiny boo-dja Koorl-bar-di wer War-dong Moorditj koo-rda,

12
Gm7 Cm7 Fm Cm7

baa lap koor- da kal- ya - koorl War-ra ke-da-la yoo-warl-koorl____

15
Fm Cm7 Fm

War-ra ke-da-la kwop koor- da_______ War-ra ke-da-la yoo-warl-koorl_

18
Cm7 Dm7(♭5) G7

— Yoo-wart moor-ditj koo - r - da! -

21
Cm7 Gm7

Bilya - k, Koorl bar-di Bar-na baal wa-ng ki-niny Nyin baal kwo-bi-dak?

24
Gm7 Cm7 Fm Cm7

Nyi-n ba-al kwo-bi-dak? Bar-na doyntj doyntj wang-ki - niny

Fm
Cm7
Fm
Cm7
27
Noo-nook boo-la kwo-bi-dak
War-dong ba-al dji-na-niny-
Instrumental
Dm7(♭5)
G7
E♭
B♭(add2)/D
Cm7
A♭
B♭
Cm7
31
Koorl-bar-di -al-i wah!
Cm7
Gm7
Cm7
37
War-dong, Koorl-bar-di
Baa-lap koom-ba ba-ka djoo
Ngar-da wer-diny ka-r-la
Gm7
Cm7
Fm
Cm7
40
Baa-lap yoo-wart kwo-bi-dak
Wa-rra ke-da-la ni - dja
Fm
Cm7
Fm
Cm7
43
Koo-ra moor-ditj ko-or- da
Bar-na wang-kiny di - ma
Dm7(♭5)
G7
E♭
B♭/D
Cm7
A♭
B♭
Cm7
47
Instrumental
A-li wah ! A-li wah !
E♭
B♭/D
Cm7
A♭
B♭
Cm7
A♭
B♭
Cm7
rit
F7/A
G/B
Cm
53

## Bilya-k

Ngalak ngarda, bilya-k koorliny
Bilya-k koorliny, ngalak warangka
Ngalak ngarda bilya-k djerabiny ngalak warangka
Bilya-k koorliny, ngalak warangka

Ngoonyoong ngankat
Ngaank ngarda djinany
Karla kaalang
Mikang-ngat koorndarm
Djinda djinany
Benang yelakitj
Koordamaart
Ngany noonook kaditjiny

Koora koora, ngalak yoowart wardan djinany
Djel bilya
Ngalak ngarda bilya-k djerabiny
Ngalak warangka
Bilya-k koorliny, ngalak warangka

Ngoonyoong ngankat
Ngaank ngarda djinany
Karla kaalang
Mikang-ngat koorndarm
Djinda djinany
Benang yelakitj
Koordamaart
Ngany noonook kaditjiny

Ngalak ngarda, bilya-k koorliny
Bilya-k koorliny, ngalak warangka
Ngalak ngarda bilya-k djerabiny ngalak warangka
Bilya-k koorliny, bilya-k koorliny
Ngalak warangka

## To the River

We go down to the river
Going to the river, we sing
We are happy down by the river we sing
Going to the river, we sing

Sweet land breeze
Watch the sun set
Fire is warm
Dreaming by moonlight
Look at the stars
Wait for tomorrow
Sweetheart
I think of you

Long ago, we didn't see the ocean
Only rivers
We are happy down by the river
We sing
Going to the river, we sing

Sweet land breeze
Watch the sun set
Fire is warm
Dreaming by moonlight
Look at the stars
Wait for tomorrow
Sweetheart
I think of you

We go down to the river
Going to the river, we sing
We are happy down by the river we sing
Going to the river, going to the river
We sing

# Bilya-k

## To the River

Arranged by Russell Holmes

Gina Williams and Guy Ghouse

**Lively** ♩ = 114 Guitar Octaves

C#m7

6
C#m7 G#7 Vocal enters C#m7

Nga - lak ngar- da, bilya - k

10
G#m7 Amaj7 C#m7 G#m7 Amaj7

koor - liny Bilya - k koor- liny, nga - lak war- ang - ka Nga - lak

13
C#m7 G#m7 Amaj7 C#m7

ngar-da bilya-k djera-biny nga lak wa -rang ka Bilya - k koor- liny, nga - lak

16
G#m7 Amaj7 F#m7

wa- rang - ka Ngoon-yoong ngan-kat Ngaank - ngarda-k

19
C#m7 F#m7

djin - any Kar - la kaa - lang Mi- kang-ngat

23
C#m7 F#m7

koo- rn - darm Djin - da dji- nany Be- nang

27
C#m7
Amaj7
3
3
ye-la - kitj K- oor - da maart Ngany noo-nook ka - ditj
32
G#9(sus4)
C#m7
G#m7
4fr
Amaj7
C#m7
iny Koo - ra koo - ra, nga - lak yoo- wart war - dan dji-nany Djel
36
G#m7
4fr
Amaj7
C#m7
G#m7
4fr
Amaj7
bi - lya Nga - lak ngar-da bilya-k djera-biny Nga-lak wa-rang ka Bilya - k
39
C#m7
G#m7
4fr
Amaj7
F#m7
koor-liny, nga - lak wa- rang - ka Ngoon-yoong ngan- kat
42
C#m7
F#m7
Ngaank ngarda-k dji - nany Kar - la kaa - lang
46
C#m7
F#m7
Mi- kang-ngat koo-rn - darm Djin-da dji-nany
50
C#m7
Amaj7
3
3
Be- nang ye-la - kitj Koor-da maart Ngany noo-nook

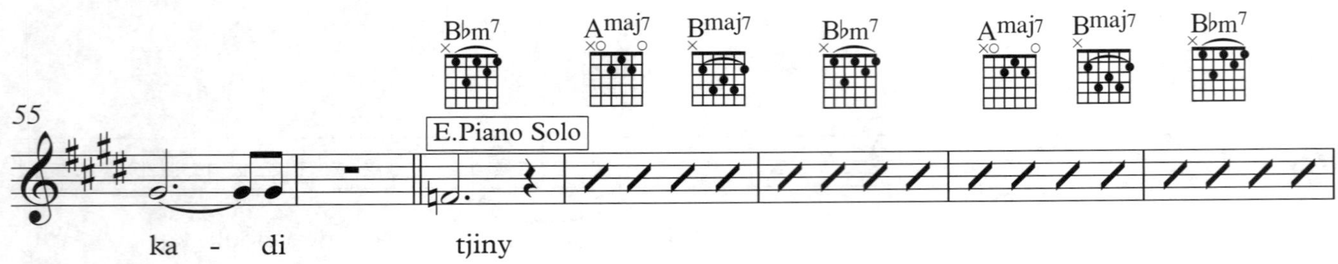
55
B♭m7
Amaj7
Bmaj7
B♭m7
Amaj7
Bmaj7
B♭m7
E.Piano Solo
ka - di
tjiny

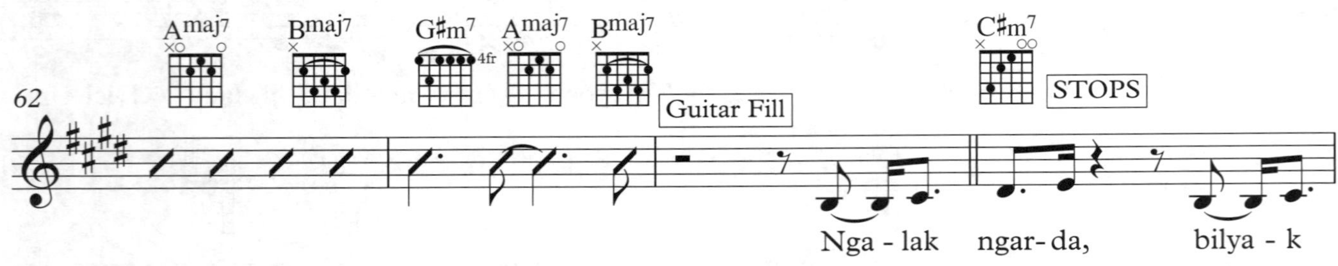
62
Amaj7
Bmaj7
G♯m7
4fr
Amaj7
Bmaj7
Guitar Fill
C♯m7
STOPS
Nga - lak ngar- da, bilya - k

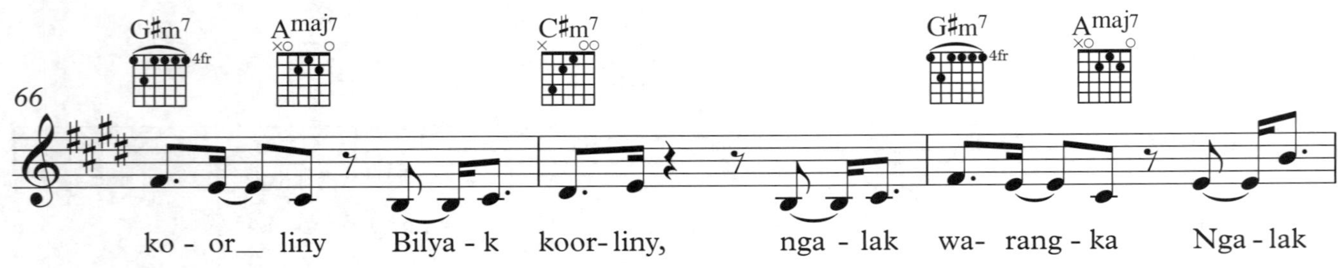
66
G♯m7
4fr
Amaj7
C♯m7
G♯m7
4fr
Amaj7
ko - or__ liny Bilya - k koor- liny, nga - lak wa- rang - ka Nga - lak

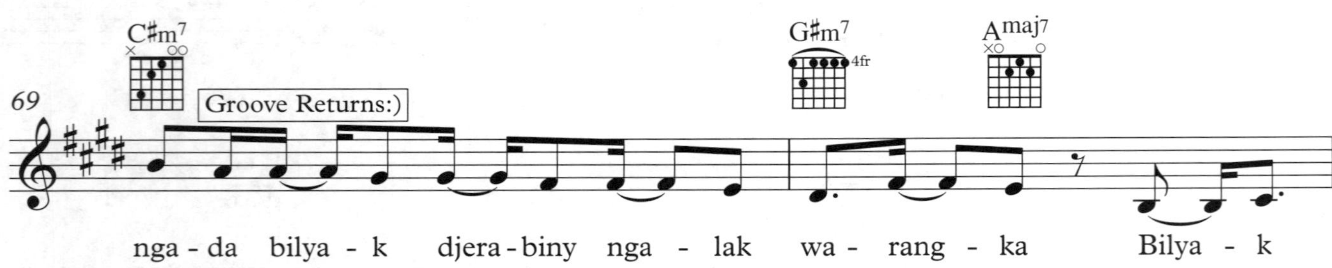
69
C♯m7
Groove Returns:)
G♯m7
4fr
Amaj7
nga - da bilya - k djera - biny nga - lak wa - rang - ka Bilya - k

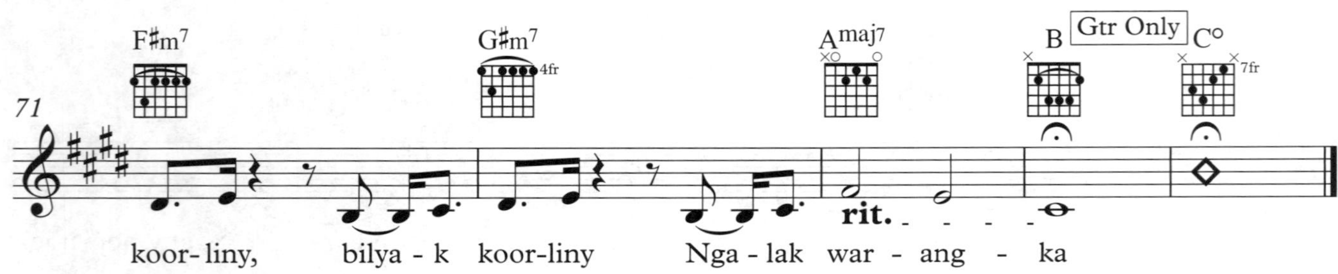
71
F♯m7
G♯m7
4fr
Amaj7
B
Gtr Only
C°
7fr
rit.
koor- liny, bilya - k koor-liny Nga - lak war - ang - ka

## Benang

Windji noonook koorliny?
Noonook yoowart kaditjiny
Windji noonook yoowarl-koorliny, yoowart koora
Windji noonook koorliny?
Noonook yoowart kaditjiny
Windji noonook yoowarl-koorliny, yoowart koora

Windji ngalang maaman?
Windji burdiya?
Ngalang koorlangka
Yoowart kaditjiny

Windji noonook koorliny?
Noonook yoowart kaditjiny
Windji noonook yoowarl-koorliny, yoowart koora
Windji noonook koorliny?
Noonook yoowart kaditjiny
Windji noonook yoowarl-koorliny, yoowart koora

Warra kedala yoowarl-koorliny
Noonar ngaank baal waahliny
Ngalang koorlangka
Yoowart djinaniny

Koorlangka nidja yoowarl-koorliny
Noonar ngaank baal waahliny
Moorditj kedala yoowarl-koorliny
Kwobidak kedala benang

Yoowart kaditjiny
Windji noonook yoowarl-koorliny, yoowart koora
Windji noonook koorliny?
Noonook yoowart kaditjiny
Windji noonook yoowarl-koorliny, yoowart koora

## Tomorrow

Where you going?
You have no idea
Where you're going, no history
Where you going?
You have no idea
Where you're going, no history

Where are our men?
Where are our bosses?
Our children
Have no idea

Where you going?
You have no idea
Where you're going, no history
Where you going?
You have no idea
Where you're going, no history

Bad days are coming
Your mothers cry
Our children
Don't see

Children, come back here
Your mothers' cry
Solid days are returning
Beautiful days tomorrow

No idea
Where you're going, no history
Where you going?
You have no idea
Where you're going, no history

# Benang

## Tomorrow

Arranged by Russell Holmes

Gina Williams and Guy Ghouse

Em7 Am7 Bm7 Cmaj7 D
ka, Yoo-wart ka - di - tjiny ooh - ooh
Em7 Bm7 Cmaj7 D Em7
Wi - ndji noo-nook koor liny? Noo-nook yoo-wart ka -di- tjiny Win-dji
Bm7 Cmaj7 D Em7
noo-nook yoo-warl koor liny, yoo - wart koo - ra Wi - ndji
Bm7 Cmaj7 D Em7
noo-nook koor liny? Noo-nook yoowart ka - di- tjiny Win - dji
Bm7 Cmaj7 D Am7
noo-nook yoo-warl koor - liny, yoo - wart koo - ra Wa - rra
Bm7 Em7 Am7
ke-da-la yoo-warl koor - liny Noo -nar
Bm7 Em7 Am7 Bm7 Em7
ngaank baal wa - ah - liny Nga -lang koor-lang - ka

Am7
Bm7
Cmaj7
D
Em
Guitar riff solo as intro
Yoo-wart djin - an - iny
Em
Em
1. 3
2.
4th time
Em
Am7
Bm7
Em7
Koor-lan-gka nidja yoo-warl koor- liny
Am7
Bm7
Em7
Am7
Noo- nar ngank baal wa - ah liny
Moor-ditj
Bm7
Em7
Am7
Bm7
ke-da-la yoo-warl- koor liny
Kwob-i - dak ke - da la
Cmaj7
D
Em7
Bm7
Cmaj7
D
be - na
ng
Yoo - wart ka-di- tjiny
Em7
Bm7
Cmaj7
D
Wi - ndji noo-nook yoo-warl-koor - liny, yoo - wart koo ra

Em7
Bm7
Cmaj7
D
Wi - ndji noo-nook koor liny? Noo-nook yo - o-wart ka - di- tjiny
Em7
Bm7
Cmaj7
D
Win - dji noo-nook yoo-warl koor liny, yoo - wart koo - ra
Em
Em
Em
Guitar riff solo as intro
Em
1.3
2.
4th time

## Wunding wer Wilara

Oh nganyang koort
Yoowart kaditj naatj kwop
Wer naatj warra
Ngany koort djel koordak noonook
Oh nganyang koort
Yoowart kaditj naatj kwop
Wer naatj warra
Ngany koort djel…

Wunding baal djeroong, baal Wilara koort barang
Baal koolark kata-ngat moort
Wilara kwobidak, Wunding koort barang
Wilara koolark burda-k moort

Oh nganyang koort
Yoowart kaditj naatj kwop
Wer naatj warra
Ngany koort djel koordak noonook
Oh nganyang koort
Yoowart kaditj naatj kwop
Wer naatj warra
Ngany koort djel…

Wunding wer Wilara baalap wort-djakoorl
Baalap moort koomba bakadjoo
Koordamaart djerabiny nyondi kaata-ngat
Kalyakoorl nyondi kaata-ngat

And I will love you till the stars fall from the sky
And I will hold you till the mountains crumble
'cause you and I were destined by the ancestors to be
Eternally

Oh nganyang koort
Yoowart kaditj naatj kwop
Wer naatj warra
Ngany koort djel koordak noonook
Oh nganyang koort
Yoowart kaditj naatj kwop
Wer naatj warra
Ngany koort djel…

## Wunding and Wilara

Oh my heart
Doesn't know what's good
Or what's bad
My heart only yearns for you
Oh my heart
Doesn't know what's good
Or what's bad
My heart only…

Wunding he was handsome, he had Wilara's heart
He lived with the hills people
Wilara was beautiful, she had Wunding's heart
Wilara lived with the valley people

Oh my heart
Doesn't know what's good
Or what's bad
My heart only yearns for you
Oh my heart
Doesn't know what's good
Or what's bad
My heart only…

Wunding and Wilara they ran away
Their families had a big fight
Sweethearts' love lost to the hills
Forever lost to the hills…

And I will love you till the stars fall from the sky
And I will hold you till the mountains crumble
'cause you and I were destined by the ancestors to be
Eternally

Oh my heart
Doesn't know what's good
Or what's bad
My heart only yearns for you
Oh my heart
Doesn't know what's good
Or what's bad
My heart only…

# Wunding wer Wilara

## Wunding and Wilara

Arranged by Russell Holmes

Gina Williams and Guy Ghouse

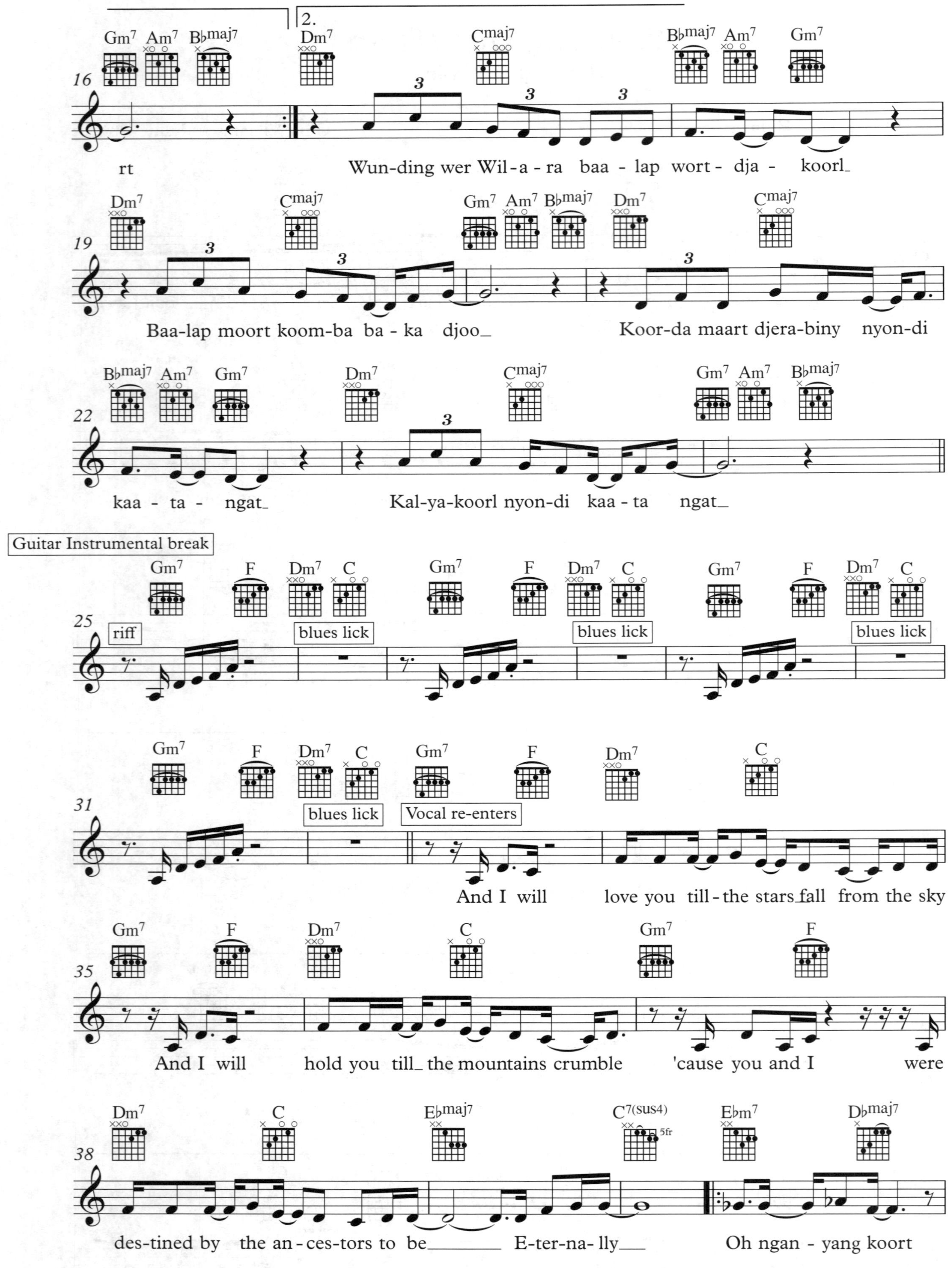
2.
Gm7 Am7 B♭maj7 Dm7 Cmaj7 B♭maj7 Am7 Gm7
rt
Wun-ding wer Wil-a-ra baa-lap wort-dja-koorl
Dm7 Cmaj7 Gm7 Am7 B♭maj7 Dm7 Cmaj7
Baa-lap moort koom-ba ba-ka djoo
Koor-da maart djera-biny nyon-di
B♭maj7 Am7 Gm7 Dm7 Cmaj7 Gm7 Am7 B♭maj7
kaa-ta-ngat
Kal-ya-koorl nyon-di kaa-ta ngat
Guitar Instrumental break
Gm7 F Dm7 C Gm7 F Dm7 C Gm7 F Dm7 C
riff
blues lick
blues lick
blues lick
Gm7 F Dm7 C Gm7 F Dm7 C
blues lick
Vocal re-enters
And I will love you till-the stars fall from the sky
Gm7 F Dm7 C Gm7 F
And I will hold you till the mountains crumble 'cause you and I were
Dm7 C E♭maj7 C7(sus4) E♭m7 D♭maj7
5fr
des-tined by the an-ces-tors to be E-ter-na-lly
Oh ngan-yang koort

42
D♭m7
A♭maj7
C♭maj7
B♭m7
Amaj7
Yoo - wart ka - ditj naatj kwop Wer naatj wa - rra Ngany koort djel
44
A♭m7
4fr
E♭m7
D♭maj7
D♭m7
A♭maj7
1.
koordak noonook Oh ngan - yang koort Yoo-wart ka - ditj naatj kwop
47
C♭maj7
B♭m7
Amaj7
E♭m7
D♭maj7
2.
Wer naatj wa - rra Ngany koort djel.. Oh ngan - yang koort

## Yeyi

Nganyang koorlangka, djaliny yeyi
Ngany nyinyak noonook
Nganyang ngaank boodja
Nganyang koorlangka, djinany yeyi
Ngany nyinyak noonook
Nganyang moyran wumbudiny

Nidja baal, nganyang kwobidak koort
Kanyiny dookaniny noonar koort
Nidja baal, nganyang kwobidak koort
Kanyiny dookaniny noonar koort

Nganyang koorlangka, koorndarm yeyi
Ngany nyinyak noonook
Nganyang karbarli kaditjiny
Nganyang koorlangka, wangkiny yeyi
Ngany nyinyak noonook
Nganyang maambart koort

Nidja baal, nganyang kwobidak koort
Kanyiny dookaniny noonar koort
Nidja baal, nganyang kwobidak koort
Kanyiny dookaniny noonar koort

Nidja baal, nganyang kwobidak koort
Kanyiny dookaniny noonar koort

## Now

My children, listen now
I give you
My mother's land
My children, look now
I give you
My grandfather's pride.

Here it is, my good heart
Keep it close to your heart
Here it is, my good heart
Keep it close to your heart

My children, dream now
I give you
My grandmother's thoughts
My children, speak now
I give you
My father's heart

Here it is, my good heart
Keep it close to your heart
Here it is, my good heart
Keep it close to your heart

Here it is, my good heart
Keep it close to your heart

# Yeyi
## Now

Arranged by Russell Holmes

Gina Williams and Guy Ghouse

Dmaj7
F°
F♯m
C♯m
10
dji - nany yeyi Ngany ny - in - yak noo - nok ngan-yang moy - ran
F♯m
D
E
12
wum-bud-iny Ni- dja ba - al ngany-ang
F♯m
D
E
A
14
kwo - bi dak koo - rt Kan-yiny doo - kan - iny noo-nar koort
D
E
F♯m
E♭m7(♭5)
17
Ni - dja ba - al, ngany- ang kwo - bi-dak koo - rt Kan -yiny

19
D
E
F♯m
C♯m
F♯m
C♯m
doo-kan-iny noo - nar koort
22
F♯m
E
D
F°
Ngan-yang koor lang - ka
ko - or - n darm yeyi Ngany nyin
24
F♯m
F°
A♭°
B°
C♯7
F♯m
E
yak noo nook ngan yang kar - bar - li ka-ditj-iny
Ngan-yang koor lang-ka
27
D
F°
F♯m
C♯m
wa-ng - kiny ye - yi Ngany nyin -yak
noo-nook ngan-yang maam - bart

F♯m D E F♯m
29
koort Ni-dja ba-al ngany-ang kwo bi-dak ko-ort
D E A D E
32
Kan-yiny dook-a- niny noo-nar koort Ni-dja ba - al, ngan-yang
F♯m E♭m7(♭5) Dmaj7 E F♯m
35
kwo - bi-dak koo-rt Kan-yiny dook-a-niny noo-nar koort
D E F♯m E♭m7(♭5) Dmaj7 E
38
rit.
Ni-dja ba - a - l kwo - bi-dak koo - rt Kan-yiny doo-ka-niny noo-nar
rit.

41
Violin
koort
F♯m
C♯m
F♯m
C♯m
F♯m
C♯m
pp
pp
45
F♯m
E
Dmaj7
E7
F♯m
E
p
48
Dmaj7
C♯m7
F♯m
E
Dmaj7
C♯m7
sfz
p

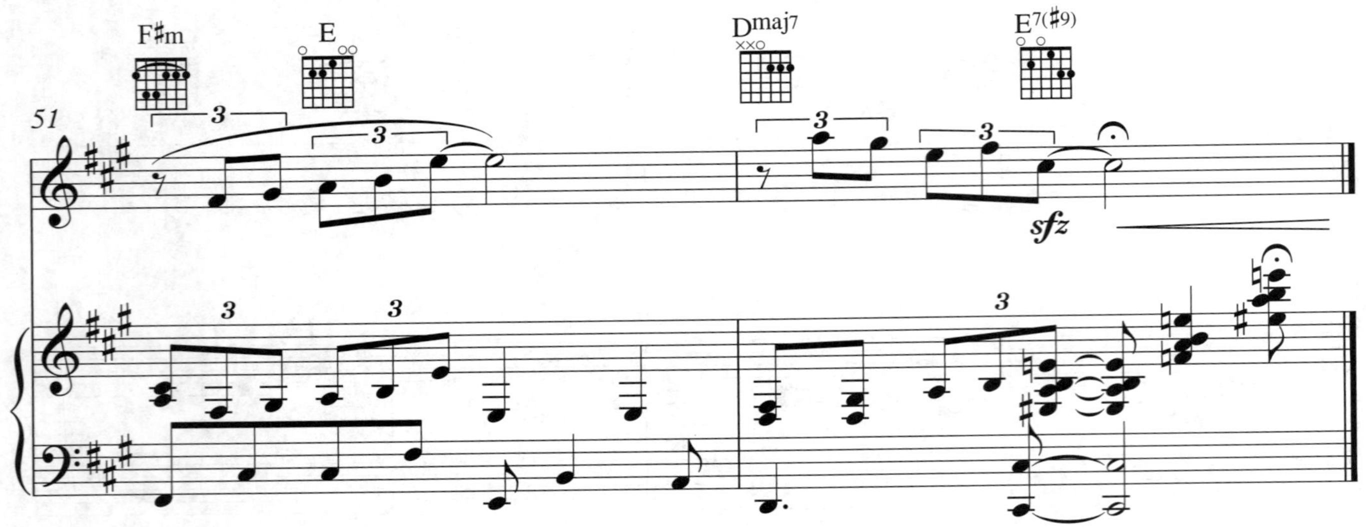

F♯m
E
Dmaj7
E7(♯9)
51
3
sfz

This is a Magabala Book

LEADING PUBLISHER OF ABORIGINAL AND
TORRES STRAIT ISLANDER STORYTELLERS.

CHANGING THE WORLD, ONE STORY AT A TIME.

First published 2021
Magabala Books Aboriginal Corporation, Broome, Western Australia Website: www.magabala.com
Email: sales@magabala.com

Magabala Books receives financial assistance from the Commonwealth Government through the Australia Council, its arts advisory body. The State of Western Australia has made an investment in this project through the Department of Local Government, Sport and Cultural Industries. Magabala Books would like to acknowledge the generous support of the Shire of Broome, Western Australia.

Magabala Books is Australia's only independent Aboriginal and Torres Strait Islander publishing house. Magabala Books acknowledges the Traditional Owners of the Country on which we live and work. We recognise the unbroken connection to traditional lands, waters and cultures. Through what we publish, we honour all our Elders, peoples and stories, past, present and future.

Edited and compiled by Gina Williams and Guy Ghouse
www.ginawilliams.com.au www.facebook.com/kalyakoorl

Arrangements by Russell Holmes
Photographs by Gareth Andersen, Tiffany Garvie, Owen Gregory and Jarred Seng



Designed by Jo Hunt
Printed and bound by Griffin Press South Australia

ISBN Print 978-1-922613-93-6
ISBN ePDF 978-1-925936-23-0

A catalogue record for this book is available from the National Library of Australia